UNIX®
FOR THE
MS-DOS USER

Kenneth Pugh

PTR Prentice Hall
Englewood Cliffs, New Jersey 07632

Library of Congress Cataloging-in-Publication Data

Pugh, Kenneth
  UNIX for the MS-DOS user / Kenneth Pugh.
    p. cm.
  Includes bibliographical references and index.
  ISBN 0-13-146077-3
  1. UNIX (Computer file) I. Title
QA76.76.063P835 1994
005.4'3--dc20   93-46801
                                        CIP

Editorial/production supervision: *Kerry Reardon*
Cover design: *Lundgren Gaphics*
Manufacturing manager: *Alexis Heydt*
Acquisitions editor: *Paul Becker*

©1994 by PTR Prentice Hall
Prentice-Hall, Inc.
A Paramount Communications Company
Englewood Cliffs, New Jersey 07632

> *This book is dedicated to Leslie Killeen for putting up with lots of*
> *computer talk over breakfast, lunch, and dinner.*
> *My thanks to Tom Truscott, a creator of Usenet, and Jon*
> *Mauney for reviewing this book.*

The publisher offers discounts on this book when ordered
in bulk quantities. For more information, contact:

        Corporate Sales Department
        PTR Prentice Hall
        113 Sylvan Avenue
        Englewood Cliffs, NJ 07632

        Phone: 201-592-2863
        Fax: 201-592-2249

Printed in the United States of America

10 9 8 7 6 5 4 3 2 1

ISBN   0-13-146077-3

Prentice-Hall International (UK) Limited, *London*
Prentice-Hall of Australia Pty. Limited, *Sydney*
Prentice-Hall Canada Inc., *Toronto*
Prentice-Hall Hispanoamericana, S.A., *Mexico*
Prentice-Hall of India Private Limited, *New Delhi*
Prentice-Hall of Japan, Inc., *Tokyo*
Simon & Schuster Asia Pte. Ltd., *Singapore*
Editora Prentice-Hall do Brasil, Ltda., *Rio de Janeiro*

CONTENTS

PROLOGUE

A few words before we begin

This book is designed to help an MS-DOS user become rapidly proficient on UNIX. The material is divided into five parts. The first part (Chapters 1 to 5) concerns operations that most MS-DOS users perform, such as copying files and editing text. The shell—the user interface to the operating system—is explored in this part. In the second part (Chapters 6 and 7) we cover the multiuser multitasking features of UNIX. In the third part (Chapters 8 to 11), we describe shell script files, which are comparable to MS-DOS batch (.bat) files. The shells include the Bourne shell, the Korn shell, and the C shell. For many common operations, the differences between them are minimal. Their programming constructs are different and that is examined in detail in this part. In the fourth part (Chapter 12) we explore the administrative side of UNIX—backing up files and setting up new users. In the fifth part (Chapters 13 to 16) we examine text-processing utilities.

The most common and useful features of the shells and tools are described in this book. A complete explanation would at least triple its size. For example, there is a large book devoted simply to how to use e-mail. If you learn the features included here, you will be able to perform all the operations you did in MS-DOS plus those available only on UNIX. You should consult the **man** pages on your system for an explanation of all the options for each program. Most sections include references to additional information.

Type Styles

The following type styles are used throughout this book:

<key>	This is a single key identifier, such as <tab>. If "control" appears, then the control key should be held down when pressing the other designated key, such as <control-C>.
<Return>	The return key. It may be labeled "Enter" or "Return" on your keyboard.
Courier italics	Replacement tokens for which you substitute your own values.
Courier bold	Commands that you type.
Courier plain	Responses from the system.
$	This is the prompt that the operating system gives. It will vary depending on the shell you are using. It may be '%' for the csh or '#' if you are logged in as the superuser.

Workout

These will give you examples to try out on your UNIX system.

Trademarks

UNIX is a trademark of UNIX Systems Laboratories.
MS-DOS is a registered trademark of Microsoft.
Windows is a trademark of Microsoft.
DESQVIEW is a registered trademark of Quarterdeck.
8086, 286, 386, 486 are trademarks of Intel.
WordPerfect is a trademark of Word Perfect Corp.
1-2-3 is a registered trademark of Lotus Corp.
Wordstar is a registered trademark of Micropro Corp.
Brief is a trademark of Underware Corp.

1 | INTRODUCTION TO UNIX

You've gotta start somewhere

UNIX is a multitasking, multiuser operating system. MS-DOS is a single-user and primarily a single-task operating system. Although they had different basic design goals, MS-DOS derived many features from UNIX. They remain distinct, but alike. A brief history of each may explain their development.

HISTORY

MS-DOS was developed over the years by a single company, Microsoft. Its original implementation appears to have been created to be compatible with the CPM operating system that ran on Z-80 microprocessors. Later development added many of the features found in UNIX, such as stream input and output.

MS-DOS runs only on Intel x86 machines (8086, 286, 386, 486, etc.). It was designed for a single user operating a single program at a time. A few multitasking features have been added, such as the print spooler. Multiple programs can exist in memory simultaneously, using the TSR (terminate and stay resident) feature. A program may execute another program (or spawn a new COMMAND.COM), but the first program must wait for the other program to finish.

Environments operating on top of MS-DOS, such as DESQVIEW and Microsoft Windows, provide multitasking capabilities. The 5.0 version of MS-DOS added system calls that aid these environments in providing multitasking. But standard MS-DOS runs only a single program at a time.

UNIX was created by Ken Thompson at AT&T in 1969. Although it was originally a single-user multitasking system, it rapidly expanded into a multiuser system. AT&T Version 6 became widely available in 1975 and was distributed to numerous universities. The Computer Science department at the University of California at Berkeley developed many new features. A split developed between the version existing at AT&T, now known as System V[1] and the one at Berkeley, now known as BSD (Berkeley Software Distribution). There are minor differences in the user interface, but substantial differences in the underlying code. A major user-interface difference was the length of filenames for the native file system, but System V Release 4.2 eliminated that difference. There are some discrepancies in the standard commands, which are noted throughout this book.

Most hardware vendors developed their own UNIX from one of these two bases.[2] Utility programs for UNIX have come from a wide variety of sources, both commercial and educational organizations. Many useful programs have been developed. However, the command options for programs are not standard, although much commonality exists.

Each UNIX version differs slightly in its implementation. Some versions combine both features of BSD and System V. The administrator of a UNIX system may make changes or additions to the system which make it appear slightly different than a standard system. The commands presented in this book are typical ones.

The basic design of UNIX was a system made up of simple tools that could be put together in complex ways. The pipe and filter method of stringing programs together was a major advancement. The tools themselves have evolved. For example, the **vi** text editor is an extension of the **ex** editor, which was originally derived from the **ed** editor.

Because UNIX was designed as a multitasking, multiuser system, many commands and programs are designed to take advantage of that feature. A single user can run multiple tasks simultaneously to take full

---

[1] System V is now maintained by UNIX System Laboratories, which is owned by Novell.

[2] Many are members of the Open Software Foundation that was formed to create a more unified standard UNIX. This and the System V standard appear to be the two major industry-wide UNIX standards that will be followed in the future. An industry movement called COSE started in 1993 to merge the user interfaces of these variant systems into a single version.

advantage of the computing power. Mail services allow users to communicate with other users.

There are several similarities in the user interface between MS-DOS and UNIX, since MS-DOS was patterned in many ways after UNIX. They both have command line interfaces, which is the focus of this book. They also have windowed interfaces (MS Windows for MS-DOS and X Windows for UNIX). Both have hierarchical file systems. Both have input/output redirection and pipes on the command line.

Many significant differences exist, mostly on the programming interface to the operating systems. Later versions of MS-DOS and new processors are erasing the differences. One major difference is the 640-kilobyte memory limitation for standard MS-DOS programs.

BASIC COMMAND OPERATION

Most of the MS-DOS commands have a counterpart in UNIX. The operation and options of the UNIX commands may be entirely different, but the results are the same. For example, to display a file in MS-DOS, you enter TYPE *FILENAME*. Under UNIX, the command **cat** *filename* does the same thing. If you entered just TYPE, MS-DOS reports an error. If you enter TYPE CON, the program uses the standard input, which is the keyboard, as the file to display. As you type each line, it will be echoed on the screen. To end the input, you type <control-Z>, which is the MS-DOS "end of file" character.

On UNIX, if you type just **cat**, the program takes its input from the standard input—the keyboard. Just as with MS-DOS, each typed line will be echoed on the screen. The keyboard "end of file" indicating character, <control-D>, ends the input.

The same program may work differently on the two systems. On MS-DOS, to display an ASCII file with pauses at the end of each page, you use MORE. Any keystroke brings up the next screen of the file. The UNIX **more**[3] has more elaborate control than MORE on MS-DOS. The implementation varies, but there are commands to view the next line (<Return>), to view the next page (<space>), and to search for a particular set of characters (/ followed by a pattern). Pattern matching is discussed in Chapter 9.

Many versions of MS-DOS have no on-line manual. UNIX has come with an on-line manual for many years. If you enter **man** *name-of-command*, the manual pages for the command will appear on your screen. If the command **man** does not work on your system, the command **help** will.

---

[3] **pg** on System V. The commands include viewing the next line (<space>), and viewing the next page (<Return>).

Executing Programs

As you try some of the workouts, you should note the differences in the way you execute programs on MS-DOS and UNIX. Program names in MS-DOS are up to eight characters long. The extension (.EXE, .COM, or .BAT) is not entered when executing a program. The characters you enter can be either lower- or upper-case. With UNIX, program names, although they can be long, tend to be terse and interesting, depending on the whim of the creator (such as **awk, grep, what, who, which**). There is no extension on program names. Names are case sensitive, so **CAT** will not execute the **cat** program.

MS-DOS and UNIX programs generally can take a filename or file specifier (one with wildcards) on the command line after the program name. Options to MS-DOS programs that alter their operation are usually listed last on the command line and are prefaced with '/' or '-'. An example of options is COPY A:ONE.DOC B:TWO.DOC /V. With UNIX, options are generally listed on the command line prefaced with a '-'. Multiple options can usually be combined after a single '-'. Options usually come immediately after the name of the program, such as **ls   -l one.doc** for a long directory listing. Options and filenames should be separated by white space (either the <space> or <tab> character).

As with MS-DOS, you can interrupt and stop programs while they are executing. The interrupt character (<control-C> on most systems) stops the program and brings you back to the command line prompt. Some MS-DOS programs, as well as UNIX programs, may be written to ignore this interrupt character and continue executing.

Workout Logging on to your system and creating files

---

1. Log onto the computer with your user name and password, which are given to you by your system administrator.

```
log in: your-login-name <Return>
password: your-password <Return> (will not be echoed)
```

If you see a message such as "Login incorrect", try reentering your name and password. If you do not have a password but the system asks for one, try just pressing <Return>. If you cannot log in, contact the system administrator.

(If you are the sole user of the system, you may be in trouble. Look through your system startup manual to see what you recorded as the password for the "root" user or superuser when you set up the system. Then log in as "root", using that password).

2. After you have logged in successfully, you may see the message of the day printed out. This "motd" is set by the system administrator in a file named "\etc\motd".

If you are using a window system, open up a terminal window to perform the exercises in this book. It may be called "Terminal Window", "Command Window", "Xterm Window," or "DECterm Window", depending on your UNIX vendor's system. Move the mouse pointer to the window and click it, so that keyboard input will be directed to that window.

3. A prompt will appear on the screen. This may be '**$**' if you are using the Bourne shell (**sh**) or the Korn shell (**ksh**), '**%**' if you are using the C Shell (**csh**), or '**#**' if you are logged in as "root". It may be something else if it has been locally defined by the system administrator. Prompts will be shown as **$** in all the examples in this book. This prompt means the same as the MS-DOS prompt.

4. Try a directory listing:

```
$ ls <Return>
```

After this example, the <Return> key will no longer be shown when entering commands at the prompt.

The prompt may appear without any intervening output. This means that there are no nonhidden files in your directory. "Hidden files" are those with names beginning with a period. Type the command with an option to list all files (including those starting with a period):

```
$ ls -a
```

You should see something similar to the following, depending on what shell you are using. Multiple names may appear on a single line. You may see many additional filenames.

```
.

..

.profile
```

or

```
.
..
.cshrc
.login
```

5. Now create a file. The command **cat > *filename*** reads the standard input (terminal keyboard) and outputs it to the standard output, which has been redirected to *filename*. If a file with the name *filename* already existed, it would be overwritten.

```
$ cat > one.doc
This is a test document numbered one<Return>
This is the second line of document one<Return>
This is a common line<Return>
<control-D>
```

Then list the file:

```
$ ls
one.doc
$
```

To display the contents of **one.doc** on the screen, type

```
$ cat one.doc
This is a test document numbered one
This is the second line of document one
This is a common line
$
```

6. Create a couple more files. Type

```
$ cat > two.doc
This is a test document numbered two<Return>
This is the second line of document two<Return>
This is a common line<Return>
<control-D>
$
```

```
$ cat > three.doc
This is a test document numbered three<Return>
This is the second line of document three<Return>
```

```
This is a common line<Return>
<control-D>
$

Then list the files. Type

$ ls
one.doc
three.doc
two.doc
$
```

7. Now try a big file. This file will be used as the data file for a number of the other workouts. In using **cat** to create a file, you will not be able to correct a mistake on a line once you have pressed the <Return> key. Do not worry about typing errors at this time. We will show how to use a UNIX text editor in a later chapter. If you do not have any mistakes, you will not have any corrections to practice on in that workout.

```
$ cat > presidents
1 Washington George
2 Adams John
3 Jefferson Thomas
4 Madison James
5 Monroe James
6 Adams John Quincy
7 Jackson Andrew
8 VanBuren Martin
9 Harrison William Henry
10 Tyler John
11 Polk James Knox
12 Taylor Zachary
13 Fillmore Millard
14 Pierce Franklin
15 Buchanan James
16 Lincoln Abraham
17 Johnson Andrew
18 Grant Ulysses Simpson
19 Hayes Rutherford Birchard
20 Garfield James Abram
21 Arthur Chester Alan
22 Cleveland Stephen Grover
```

```
23 Harrison Benjamin
24 Cleveland Stephen Grover
25 McKinley William
26 Roosevelt Theodore
27 Taft William Howard
28 Wilson Thomas Woodrow
29 Harding Warren Gamaliel
30 Coolidge John Calvin
<control-D>
$
```

8. You should change your password the first time you log in and every few months thereafter. This helps but does not absolutely guarantee that another user will not be able to forge your identity.

   The requirements for your password differ on the system. On BSD, the minimum length is four characters or six characters if it consists of only upper- or lowercase letters. On System V, the minimum is six characters and it must contain one numeric and two alphabetic characters. It must also differ from old password by some characters. Type

   ```
   $ passwd
   Enter new password: new-password
   Reenter new password: new-password
   $
   ```

   If you get a message such as "Doesn't match—try again", your two typings did not match. If the prompt reappears, your new password is accepted. Remember your new password. The system administrator cannot determine what it is. However, he/she can change it. On some systems, you may need to use **yppasswd** to change your password. This works in the same way as **passwd**.

9. Logging out. You should log out before leaving your terminal. Type

   ```
   $ <control-D>    (if you are using sh or ksh)
   $ logout         (if you are using csh)
   ```

   Note that <control-D> should work with any shell. The C shell variable **ignoreeof** may be set, so that <control-D> does not work. This variable is discussed in Chapter 11.

Help

As noted previously, the manual pages for UNIX commands are kept on-line. The pages consist of the headings, which may include the following:

Name	Name and summary
Synopsis	Usage with the options
Description	Details on usage
Files	Other files used with the command
See also	Related information and commands
Diagnostics	Values of exit codes and potential errors
Examples	Some examples of usage
Bugs	Known bugs, if any
Restrictions	Limitations
Authors	Who wrote the program

In the synopsis, a standard convention is followed. Square brackets ([ ]) surround optional arguments. Ellipses (...) show where repeated arguments are permitted. Italics or underlines are used for the names of arguments for which a particular name is to be substituted.

It is possible when you look for help, you may run across a command that does not seem correct. There can be multiple entries that have the same name. Although you cannot see easily on-line, these entries are from different sections of the manual. The section number is listed in parentheses after the item name. The organization of the entire manual varies, but a typical one has such sections as:

Commands	Section 1
System calls	Section 2
Subroutines	Section 3
Special files	Section 4
File format	Section 5
Packages	Section 7
Maintenance	Section 8

If you need to look up an item in a particular section, you can use

man *section-number item*

such as

man 2 open

There is no easy way to find out exactly what command might be available to do a particular operation. Some paper manuals have permuted indexes. Many UNIX systems have a **-k** option available on **man**. The syntax is

```
man -k keyword
```

You replace *keyword* with the word you are looking for. For example,

```
man -k files
```

will list names and summaries of all commands that have the string **files** in the summary.

Errors

With many commands you get a "Usage" message if you do not type in required arguments. This message gives a brief summary of the command line arguments. On other commands, the command by itself has default values it uses if you do not enter anything but the command name.

Workout man

---

1. Look up help for **ls**.

   ```
   $ man ls
   ```

   If this command does not work, try **help ls**.
2. Scroll through the help using <space> to go to the next page and <Return> to go to the next line.
3. Look up help for **man**.

   ```
   $ man man
   ```

4. While looking at the **man** description, search for particular words by using **/word**. Type

   ```
   /Files
   ```

5. You can exit either by scrolling to the end or by typing the interrupt character (<control-C>).

FOR FURTHER INFORMATION

AT&T. 1988. *UNIX System V/386 User's Guide*. Englewood Cliffs, N.J.: Prentice Hall. Some step-by-step exercises through UNIX programs.

AT&T. 1988. *UNIX System V/386 User's Reference*. Englewood Cliffs, N.J.: Prentice Hall. The manual pages for UNIX programs.

Coffin, Stephen. 1990. *UNIX System V Release 4: The Complete Reference*. McGraw Hill.

Gilly, Daniel, and O'Reilly staff. 1992. *UNIX in a Nutshell*. O'Reilly.

Heslop, Brent, and David Angell. 1990. *Mastering SunOS*. Sybex.

Libes, Don, and Sandy Ressler. 1989. *Life with UNIX*. Englewood Cliffs, N.J.: Prentice Hall. Sources for applications, user groups, and so on.

Lomuto, A., and N. Lamuto. 1983. *A UNIX Primer*. Englewood Cliffs, N.J.: Prentice Hall. Introduction for beginners.

Sobell, Mark G. 1989. *A Practical Guide to the UNIX System*. Menlo Park, Calif.: Benjamin-Cummings. This is a more detailed overview of many of the UNIX commands.

Waite, Mitchell, Donald Martin, and Stephen Prata. 1992. *The Waite Group's UNIX System V Primer*. Sams.

COMMAND SUMMARY

Typing a file	**cat** *filename(s)*
Typing a file with pauses	**more** *filename*
	pg *filename*
Copying a file from keyboard	**cat >** *filename*
	end with <control-D>
Listing a directory	**ls**
Include hidden files	**-a**
Help	**man** *name-of-command*
	help *name-of-command*
Changing your password	**passwd**
Logging out	**<control-D>** (sh, ksh)
	logout (csh)

2 | FILES AND DIRECTORIES

Everything has to be kept somewhere so that you can find it

MS-DOS files and UNIX files are used for the same purposes—to hold executable programs and data. The filename structure differs between the two systems. The MS-DOS directory organization corresponds approximately to UNIX directory organization, with some differences in detail.

FILES

File Types

Just as in MS-DOS, files in UNIX contain both executable programs and data. Program files in both systems contain machine language instructions to the processor. They are unreadable to anyone other than an experienced programmer on the particular hardware.

Data files contain information such as the text of a word processor document or the records in a mailing list. The former is usually a text (ASCII) file and the latter is a binary file. MS-DOS treats text files and binary data files differently. A text file contains ASCII characters with a <control-Z> character designating the end of the file. Text manipulations of the file (such as TYPE) will stop at the <control-Z>, even if the file contains more bytes. Lines in a text file are kept as two characters—a <carriage-return> followed by a <line-feed>. Binary files do not have an end-of-file character. They are not organized as lines. They may contain non-ASCII characters. If you try to TYPE them, garbage characters may appear on the screen.

UNIX makes no distinction between text and binary data files. There is no end-of-file character kept in the file. The number of bytes in the file is its length. You type a <control-D> to signify the end of keyboard input, but this character is not part of the file. If the file contains text data, each line ends with a single character, a <line-feed>, also known as a <new-line>.

If you have MS-DOS ASCII text files that you want to transfer to UNIX, the end-of-line characters must be translated from the two-character to the single-character version. Many UNIX systems provide a utility to perform this conversion. In Chapter 9, you will learn how to write one yourself.

Filenames

MS-DOS has two parts to a filename: an eight-character name and a three-character extension. The extension is used by the operating system to identify executable files (".EXE" and ".COM"). The extension is also used to identify batch files (".BAT"), which are text files containing commands. Programs such as WordPerfect and Lotus 1-2-3 use the extension (.DOC, .WKS) to identify which data files contain information created by that particular program.

UNIX filenames can be up to 255 characters long.[1] There is no separate extension to the name. Executable files are identified by the file permission, which is described in the next section. An executable file may have any name. Names can include a period. Some programs use the part of the name following the period as an extension. For example, '.c' is used for C language source files.

A UNIX filename can contain any characters except '/'. However, it is best to use only the alphabetic characters and digits and a few symbols, such as '-', '_', and '.'. Unlike MS-DOS, filenames are case sensitive. You can have files named "one.doc", "One.doc", "ONe.doc", and so on, in the same directory. Using capitalization alone to distinguish between files is not advisable. Most UNIX commands use lowercase names.

File Attributes

Each file in MS-DOS has several attributes. The ones that have comparable usage on UNIX are "Read only" and "Hidden". The former states that a file cannot be written to or erased. The latter prevents the file from appearing on directory listings.

---

[1] In versions of System V prior to Release 4.2, the filename limit was 14 characters.

The other MS-DOS file attributes have nothing comparable. The "Archive" attribute is set by the backup program to show that a file has been backed up. Backup under UNIX uses a different organization, which we cover in Chapter 12. "System" attribute shows that a file is used by MS-DOS. Under UNIX, the system itself is in the root directory.

On UNIX, file access is assigned to three sets of users: the individual owner of the file, the group that owns the file, and the rest of the world of users. Groups and the world are discussed in Chapter 6. Each set of users has permissions for reading, writing, and executing a particular file. A file can have any combination of the three permissions. They are designated on the directory listings and commands as 'r' (read) , 'w' (write), and 'x' (execute).

The permissions are set when the file is created.[2] The **chmod** command changes the permissions for a file or set of files. Its syntax is

```
chmod u+[rwx] file-name(s)
chmod u-[rwx] file-names(s)
```

You specify the set, such as 'u' for you, the individual user. Adding a permission for a file requires the '+' symbol. Deleting a permission requires the '-' symbol. For example,

```
chmod u-w one.doc
```

deletes your write permission for the **one.doc** file. This makes the file read-only. The command

```
chmod u+w one.doc
```

adds write permission for you for the **one.doc** file.

The corresponding hidden attribute in UNIX is not based on an attribute of the file, but on the name. Hidden files in UNIX are those whose names start with a period. These files do not appear on the directory listing created by **ls**, unless the **-a** option is used.

Listing Directories

In MS-DOS, the DIR command defaults to listing the files in the current directory. You can specify a filename, and it will list only that file-

---

[2] The **umask** command changes the default manner in which the attributes are set. This command is discussed in Chapter 6.

name. If you specify a name with wildcards (e.g., '*' and '?'), only files whose names match that pattern will be listed. If the specified filename is a directory, the files in that directory will be listed. Each file is listed with its name, its size in bytes, and the date and time it was last modified. If the file is a directory, its size is shown as "<DIR>".

In UNIX, the directory listing command is `ls`. By default, it lists only the names of the files in the current directory. If you give it the option `-l` (for "long"), it lists more information about each file. In later chapters we discuss some of this information. The most important ones for now are the type of the file, the permissions, the name of the owner, the size in bytes, and the date and time.

Files you create are usually either directories or ordinary files. An ordinary file can contain a program or data. The first character in the listing is '-' for ordinary files and 'd' for directories. The next nine characters give the permissions for the file. The first three of these characters designate the read, write, and execute permissions for the user who is the owner. They are specified as 'r' (read), 'w' (write), and 'x' (execute) if the corresponding permission is granted, and as '-', if not.

The name of the owner shown is the log-in name. The size in bytes and the date and time mean the same as in MS-DOS. They are the number of bytes in the file and the date and time the file was last modified or created. The name of the file appears on the right of the listing.

Like MS-DOS, you can list a particular file in a directory by specifying the filename with the `ls` command. Filenames with wildcards are examined in the next section. If the filename is a directory, `ls` lists the files in that directory. You can list all the files in all subdirectories with the `-R` (recursive) option.

Workout Directory listing

---

1. Try a directory listing of your home directory:

```
$ ls -al
```

You should be able to pick out the permissions, size, owner, date, time, and names of each file.

2. Try a directory listing of your parent directory:

```
$ ls -l ..
```

If the list scrolls by on the screen too fast to read, type the following for BSD:

```
$ ls -l .. | more
```

or for System V:

```
$ ls -l .. | pg
```

If you are on a multiuser system, you will notice that there are a number of directories, each owned by different users.

3. Change the permissions on **one.doc** to disallow reading and then list the file.

```
$ chmod u-r one.doc
$ ls -l one.doc
```

4. Try to read the file.

```
$ cat one.doc
one.doc: Permission denied
```

You get an error message, since you do not have read permission. The text of the message may vary on your system.

5. Change the permission to disallow writing and list the file to see how the permission has changed.

```
$ chmod u-w one.doc
$ ls -l one.doc
```

6. Try to write to it.

```
$ cat > one.doc
one.doc: cannot create
```

You get the error message because you do not have write permission. The text of the message may vary on your system.

If you are using the csh, you may get a message as "File exists". In that case, type

```
$ unset noclobber
```

and retry

```
$ cat > one.doc
```

Then type

```
set noclobber
```

7. Now change the privileges back to what they were and list it again.

```
$ chmod u+rw one.doc
$ ls -l one.doc
```

Filename Pattern Matching

In MS-DOS, you can specify wildcard characters in filenames when using the DIR command and a few other commands, such as COPY. The wildcards include a '?' for any single character and a '*' for a group of any characters. If you specify a '.', it is treated as a separator between the name and the extension. For example, DIR *.DOC will list all files whose extension is "DOC". Wildcards cannot be used with every command. For example, if you type TYPE *.DOC, an error is reported.

You can use similar wildcard characters for UNIX filenames.[3] '?' matches any single character. '*' matches a group of characters. Unlike MS-DOS, the '*' can appear before and/or after a string of characters. Any other non-wildcard characters (including the period '.') must be matched exactly. For example:

*	Matches all filenames in directory
.	Matches any filename with a period in the name
..*	Matches filenames such as "a.b.c" and "abc.def.ghi"
*xyz	Matches filenames such as "xyz" and "abcxyz"

The shell provides an advanced form of pattern matching that uses sets of characters. You specify a set by enclosing a list of characters within square brackets ([and]). A matching name must match one of the charac-

---

[3] Keep in mind that the shell pattern-matching syntax shown here is different from the pattern-matching syntax of the **grep** utility described in Chapter 9. The two use the same characters for different purposes.

ters in the set. A hyphen can be used to specify a range of characters (in ASCII order) without having to list them all. For example:

[abc]	Matches **a** or **b** or **c**
[a-z]	Matches **a** or **b** or **c** or **d**, and so on
doc[0-9]	Matches **doc0** or **doc1** or **doc2**, and so on
[Aa]dd	Matches **useradd** or **User-Add**, and so on
[Aa][Dd][Dd]	Matches **userADD** or **xxxAdd**, and so on

There is a significant difference between MS-DOS and UNIX in the way that filename pattern matching works. With MS-DOS, each individual command interprets the pattern match. If the command is not designed to match patterns, it fails.

In UNIX, the command interpreter, the shell, performs the pattern matching on the command line that you type. The shell passes to the program a new command line with the names of the matching files substituted for the pattern. Many programs are written to operate on multiple filenames passed to them on the command line. For example, if you typed

```
$ cat *.doc
```

the shell finds the matching filenames and calls **cat** with the line

```
cat one.doc two.doc three.doc
```

The **cat** program outputs every file whose name is passed to it.

This is a significant difference from the way in which MS-DOS operates. If you tried TYPE *.DOC, you get a command error, since TYPE cannot find a file called "*.DOC". On the other hand, some MS-DOS commands do interpret wildcards. Suppose that you typed COPY *.COM A: in MS-DOS. The COPY command gets two arguments: "*.COM" and "A:". It looks up each filename matching "*.COM" and copies that file to the A drive.

Copying Files

With MS-DOS, you can specify the copying of files in a number of ways. You can copy a single file to another file; a single file to another directory; a set of files specified with wildcards to another directory; and a set of files to another set, both specified with wildcards. Of these four ways, the first three are available with the UNIX copy command (**cp**). For the last operation, you will need to write a shell script, as described in Chapter 8.

The syntax for copying files is somewhat like MS-DOS:

```
cp source destination
```

and

```
cp source(s) destination-directory
```

The *destination* can be either a filename or a directory name. If you name multiple files as the source, the destination must be a directory. For example, you can copy **one.doc** to **another.doc** with

```
cp one.doc another.doc
```

To copy **one.doc** to another directory (say **/other**), you can use either

```
cp one.doc /other/one.doc
```

or

```
cp one.doc /other
```

To copy two files to the **/other** directory, you enter

```
cp one.doc two.doc /other
```

Since the shell expands wildcards, then

```
cp *.doc /other
```

works as if you had typed

```
cp one.doc two.doc three.doc /other
```

Renaming or Moving a File

With MS-DOS, you rename a file with the RENAME command. With UNIX, the **mv** command performs the same operation.

```
mv old-name new-name
```

The **mv** command is used both for renaming a file and for moving a file to a different directory. The **mv** command renames a file if *new-name* specifies the same directory as *old-name*. For example,

```
mv another.doc still-another.doc
```

renames **another.doc** to **still-another.doc**. If a file with the name *new-name* already exists and that file is not read-only, **mv** replaces that file with *old-name*.

mv moves the file to another directory if *new-name* is in a different directory than *old-name*. For example

```
mv another.doc /other/another.doc
```

moves **another.doc** to the **/other** directory and gives it the name **another.doc**. MS-DOS does not have a comparable command, although a batch file could be written to do this.

Deleting a File

The MS-DOS ERASE or DEL commands delete a single file or multiple files. If you used the "/P" option, you will get a prompt for the deletion of each file. If the file specification is "*.*", you are automatically asked if you want to delete everything in the directory.

The corresponding UNIX command is **rm.** You can erase a single file or multiple files. There is no confirmation if you specify every file in the entire directory with "*". However, the interactive option (**-i**) can be used to prompt for each deletion. The syntax is

```
rm filename(s)
```

To delete a single file, you specify the name, as

```
rm another.doc
```

To delete multiple files, you can either use wildcards or you can specify them explicitly

```
rm another.doc still-another.doc
```

or

```
rm *another.doc
```

To erase everything in the directory with prompting, use

```
rm -i *
```

If you do not have write permission for a file, the **rm** command will prompt you before removing it, regardless of whether you use the **-i** option. You can turn off this prompting with the **-f** option.

Combining Files

You combine files in MS-DOS with the COPY command by using a wildcard specification for the source and a filename for the destination. You may have accidentally done this if you misspelled a destination directory. You can also combine files by using the '+' symbol between the source filenames.

The UNIX `cat` command performs the equivalent operation. The files specified on the command are output sequentially to the standard output, the terminal screen. You redirect this output to a file to do the combining. For example,

```
cat one.doc two.doc three.doc > all.doc
```

copies the contents of the three files to "all.doc".

Printing Files

To print an ASCII file under MS-DOS, you enter either TYPE *FILE-NAME* > PRN or PRINT *FILENAME*. This may print the file immediately or place it in a queue for printing. Under UNIX the command to perform printing is

```
lp filename
```

On some systems, you need to use `lpr` *filename* instead. The file is placed on a queue for printing.

Your system may require options with `lp` and `lpr` to tell it which printer to use. Check with your system administrator.

Workout Files

1. Copy a file.

   ```
   $ cp one.doc another.doc
   ```

2. Do a directory listing to see the new file.

```
$ ls
...
another.doc
...
```

3. Rename the new file.

```
$ mv another.doc still-another
```

4. Do a listing to see the new name.

```
$ ls
...
still-another
...
```

5. Remove the new file.

```
$ rm still-another
```

6. Do a listing to see that the file is gone.

```
$ ls
```

7. Try printing a file.

```
$ lp one.doc
or
$ lpr one.doc
```

Depending on your system, you may see no response to this command or you may see an indication that the printing has been queued, such as "job *number*". If you have more then one printer on your system, check with your system administrator to determine which one is the default printer.

DIRECTORIES

Both UNIX and MS-DOS have a hierarchical file system. Every system has a root directory with subdirectories that may have subdirectories within them. The basic notational difference is that MS-DOS uses a back slash ('\')

as the root directory and directory separator and UNIX uses the forward slash ('/'), which is used for options by MS-DOS.

An important navigational difference is that with MS-DOS, you start out in the root directory, unless the AUTOEXEC.BAT is set to change to another directory. With UNIX, your home directory is a subdirectory. Depending on how your system is set up, it might be **/usr/users/***your-user-name* or **/usrs/***your-user-name*. You can find out what it is by typing **pwd** (print working directory) just after you log in. Typically, you keep all your personal files in your home directory or subdirectories of it.

If a pathname on MS-DOS starts with a "\", the pathname is relative to the root directory. If it does not start with a "\", it is relative to the current directory. This works the same way in UNIX with the exception that the character is "/". Similar to MS-DOS, a single period "." represents the current directory. A double period ".." represents the parent directory of the current directory.

MS-DOS has disk specifiers, such as "A:", "B:", "C:". These designate either a different physical disk or a different partition of a fixed disk. Each disk has its own root directory. UNIX has only a single root directory, regardless of the number of physical disks. The other disks or disk partitions are referenced as subdirectories in the root directory. This is done by a process called "mounting", which is described in Chapter 12. The typical user does not need to be concerned with the mounting process.

Standard Directories

MS-DOS has no standard directories. The operating system files are typically in a directory named "\DOS". Commercial programs are kept in directories that are designated at installation. For example, WordPerfect programs may be kept in "\WP51" and Lotus programs may be kept in "\123". You usually keep data files in your own directories (say, \MY-DOCS) or in subdirectories of a program directory (e.g., \WP51\MY-DOCS).

In UNIX the directory structure between versions varies, but it tends to have a similar organization. User directories, such as your home directory, are kept in **/usr/users** or a similarly named directory. User programs (such as WordPerfect) might be kept in **/usr/bin**. Standard programs that come with the operating system are stored in **/bin**. Temporary files are usually written to the **/tmp** directory. Two standard directories that are of importance to the administrator are **/etc** for configuration programs and data and **/dev** for devices.

Directory Commands

Since MS-DOS and UNIX both have hierarchical file structures, they have similar sets of commands. To change the current directory, you use **cd**; to

make a directory, you use **mkdir**; and to remove a directory, you use **rmdir**.
On both systems, to remove a directory it must be empty except for the "."
(current directory) and ".." (parent directory) entries. There is one major difference in the commands. Under MS-DOS, CD with no parameters prints out the
current directory. Under UNIX, **cd** changes the current directory to your home
directory. The UNIX **pwd** command prints the current directory.

Workout Directories

---

1. Find your home directory. To be sure that you are in your home
   directory, type

   ```
   $ cd
   ```

   Then use the "print working directory" command:

   ```
   $ pwd
   /usr/users/your-user-name
   ```

   The pathname may differ from that shown, depending on your system.
2. Go up one level, print that directory, and list its contents.

   ```
   $ cd ..
   $ pwd
   /usr/users
   $ ls
   ... (login-ids of the other users)
   ```

3. Go up another level and print that directory.

   ```
   $ cd ..
   $ pwd
   /usr
   ```

   If you only had two directory names in your home directory (such
   as "/home/your-user-name"), the **pwd** command will print out
   "/".
4. Go to the root directory and list the contents.

   ```
   $ cd /
   ```

```
$ ls
... (names of the subdirectories in the root directory)
```

5. Switch to the program directory and list what is in that directory.

```
$ cd bin
$ ls
... (names of programs)
```

6. Now switch back to your home directory.

```
$ cd
```

7. Make a subdirectory, switch to it, and list it.

```
$ mkdir data
$ cd data
$ ls
```

8. Nothing will appear, as a directory is created with only two entries in it ("." and ".."). These are not output by the standard `ls` command. Try

```
$ ls -a
.
..
```

9. Copy the ".doc" files in your home directory to this directory. Then list the files.

```
$ cp ../*.doc .
$ ls
```

10. Switch back to your home directory and list the files in the **data** subdirectory.

```
$ cd ..
$ ls data
... (filenames)
```

11. Try listing a file that does not exist:

```
$ cat xxxxxxx
cat: xxxxxxx: no such file or directory
```

The text of the error message may vary on your system.

FOR FURTHER INFORMATION

Nutshell Handbooks. 1987. *UNIX in a Nutshell, Berkeley Edition.* Sebastopol, Calif.: O'Reilly and Associates.

Nutshell Handbooks. 1987. *UNIX in a Nutshell, System V Edition.* Sebastopol, Calif.: O'Reilly and Associates.

COMMAND SUMMARY

Changing permissions on files	**chmod** *permissions filename(s)*
Listing files	**ls** *filename(s)*
Long listing	`-l`
Hidden files	`-a`
All subdirectories	`-R`
Copying files	**cp** *source(s) destination*
Renaming a file	**mv** *old-name new-name*
Moving a file	**mv** *old-name destination*
Deleting a file	**rm** *filenames*
Printing a file	**lp** *filename*
	or
	lpr *filename*
Changing directories	**cd** *directory*
Changing to home directory	**cd**
Making a directory	**mkdir** *directory*
Removing a directory	**rmdir** *directory*
Printing working directory	**pwd**
Filename pattern matching	
Any single character	?
Any group of characters	*
Sets of characters	[ ]

3 | THE USER INTERFACE: THE SHELL

Someone to carry out your every command

The shell is your user interface to UNIX. You may be using the Bourne shell, the C shell, the Korn shell, or another variant. The shells provide command execution features as well as their own programming language, similar to the MS-DOS COMMAND.COM program.

SHELLS

In MS-DOS the COMMAND.COM program is the standard user interface to the operating system. Some vendors supply alternative COMMAND.COM programs that have additional features. In either case, COMMAND.COM reads the keys that you type and then executes programs or performs operations based on your input. Some of the commands it performs internally are DIR, DELETE, COPY, TIME, and DATE. If the name you type is not an internal command, COMMAND.COM attempts to execute a program by that name. It first looks for an .EXE or a .COM file that matches the name, then for a .BAT (batch) file that matches. If there is a path (i.e., one or more directories) in the name, COMMAND.COM looks only in that directory for a match. If there is not a path in the name, it first searches the current directory. If it does not find a match there, it looks at the PATH environment variable and examines all the directories listed.

When COMMAND.COM finds the matching program file, it loads and executes the program. COMMAND.COM waits until the program is finished and then starts accepting input from the keyboard again. You may type arguments after the program name, such as WP MY-DOC.DOC. COMMAND.COM passes these arguments to the program. Some programs read these arguments and treat them as files to be operated upon. Some of the arguments may start with "/" or "-", such as COPY ONE.DOC A: /V. These symbols are usually used to specify options that make a program perform its operations in a different way.

With UNIX, the program that provides the user interface is called a shell. There are three common shells that provide similar services: the Bourne shell (**sh**), the C shell (**csh**), and the Korn shell (**ksh**). The Bourne and C shells have slightly different syntax for some standard shell features. The C shell has some additional features, which include command history. The Korn shell has much the same syntax as the Bourne shell, with many of the features of the C shell.

The operation of the shells parallels the MS-DOS COMMAND.COM. They read the keys that you type and then execute programs or functions. Each shell performs only a few commands internally (such as **cd**). For other input, it looks for a file that matches the name you typed. As noted in the section on filenames, there are no standard extensions that designate executable files. If there is a path in the name, it looks only in that directory for a match. If there is not a path in the name, it looks at the environment variable named **PATH** and examines all the directories listed.[1] The current directory ('.') is usually included in the **PATH** variable. However, the current directory will not be searched if it is not included in **PATH**. If a file with the name given is not found, the shell will respond "xxx: not found", where xxx is what you typed. If there is a file by the given name but you do not have execute permission for it, the shell responds "xxx: permission denied". The text of these messages may be different on your system.

The shell waits until the executing program finishes and then starts accepting input again from the keyboard. Since UNIX is multitasking, you can tell the shell to execute the program in the background and to continue to accept input from you. This feature is described in Chapter 8.

The shell passes the arguments to the program executed. Before it does, it expands arguments that have wildcards in them (such as ***.doc**). If there is more than one matching filename, the program will get more arguments than you typed. If you do not want the shell to expand an argument

---

[1] In actuality, the shells set an appropriate shell variable from this environment variable and use that shell variable instead. Shell variables are discussed in Chapter 8.

containing wildcard characters, you should surround the characters with quotation marks. For example,

```
$ cat "*.doc"
```

will output a file called ***.doc** to the screen. Like MS-DOS, arguments beginning with '-' are usually reserved for options to programs. However, options are typically specified immediately after the program name on the command line, before any filenames.

INPUT KEYS

As you type characters to the shell or a program, UNIX stores them in a buffer until you complete the line by hitting the <Return> or <Enter> key. Then the entire string is passed to the shell or program. Until you have completed the line, you can edit the string using some editing characters.

The key to erase the preceding character (**erase**) is either <back-space>, <delete>, or <control-H>, depending on how your terminal is set up. The key to erase the entire line (or **kill** key) is usually <control-U>. Your keys may be different, depending on how your system administrator has set up your account.

The escape character is the '\' key. If you type this key, the immediately succeeding key is not interpreted as a key with any particular meaning. For example, \<**Return**> is not treated as the end of the line, but that you wish to continue the command to the next line. The \<**delete**> will not delete a character, but may produce "^?" on the screen, depending on your system.

Special Keys

With MS-DOS, you can interrupt the executing program with the <control-C> or the <control-break> key, unless the program has turned off that capability. Under UNIX, you can interrupt a program with the inter-rupt key (termed the **intr** key), which is usually set to <control-C>. Each program can turn off this capability. You can also use the **quit** key, which is usually <control-\>, to stop an executing program. If you use that key to end a program, a special file is created that is an image of the executing process. This file is named **core**. This file can be examined by a programmer with debugging tools to determine what was occurring in the program when you stopped it. You should not normally use the **quit** key to termi-nate a process, as the **core** file can be quite large. Like MS-DOS, you can stop output to the terminal screen with the **stop** key, <control-S>, and restart output with the **start** key, <control-Q>.

Setting the Input Keys

If you want to change the settings of editing and special keys, use the `stty` command. Typing `stty` all by itself outputs the current settings. On some systems, you may need to type `stty all` or `stty-a` to get all the settings. You can change the key used for a particular purpose with

    stty purpose new-character

The *purpose* is any key that was described in the preceding two sections (e.g., **erase**). The *new-character* may be specified with the actual key. If the character is a control character, you can also specify it with ^*character*. For example, to change the erase key to <control-G>, enter

    stty erase<control-G>

or

    stty erase ^G

The **stty** command can also set other items concerning the state of the terminal input and output, such as the baud rate for connections via modem. Check the **man** pages for all the details.

Workout Shell

---

1. Find out the editing and special characters for your terminal.

    $ stty

   If this does not list the characters, try

    $ stty all

   or

    $ stty -a

2. Then try

    $ lsxxxx

You should get back a message "lsxxxxx: Command not found", or something similar.

3. Type

```
$ lsxxxx
```

Before hitting the <Enter> or <Return> key, use the character-erase key, as shown by **stty** (<backspace>, <delete>, or <control-H>) to erase the x's. Then hit the <Enter> or <Return> key and you will get a directory listing.

4. Type

```
$ lsxxxx
```

Before hitting the <Enter> or <Return> key, use the line erase key <control-U> to erase the entire line. Then enter

```
$ ls *.doc
```

You should get a directory listing that includes

```
one.doc
three.doc
two.doc
```

5. Type

```
$ ls "*.doc"
```

You should not get any listing. The prompt just reappears.

6. Type

```
$ echo $PATH
```

You will get a line showing the current path. $ precedes the name of variable, such as **PATH,** when its value is to be used.

7. If you do not like the key settings, change them. For example, change the kill-a-line character with

```
$ stty kill ^K
```

ENVIRONMENT AND SHELL VARIABLES

MS-DOS has environment variables that COMMAND.COM and other programs may query for values. You set an environment variable by typing "*name=value*". The most common MS-DOS variables are PROMPT (what to output for the COMMAND.COM prompt), PATH (where to look for programs), and COMSPEC (where to find COMMAND.COM). Many other variables are used by vendor programs.

UNIX also has environment variables that are used in much the same way as MS-DOS environment variables. There are also shell variables, which are used mainly for shell scripts but which do not get exported to spawned programs. Shell variables are covered in Chapter 8.

Some of the standard environment variables are **MAIL**, the filename for your mail, and **SHELL**, the default shell. The **TERM** variable is the type of terminal. These variables are usually set up in your log-in script.

How you set the values of the environment variables depends on the shell you are using. The Bourne and Korn shells use

```
$ name=value
$ export name
```

The first statement sets a shell variable to the value given. The **export** statement makes an environment variable with the same name and value as the shell variable. On most versions of the Bourne shell, the **printenv** command lists the environment variables. On others, the **export** command without any arguments lists the environment variables.

Under the C shell, the syntax to set an environment variable is

```
$ setenv name value
```

To print out the values, you use

```
$ printenv
```

With either shell, if *value* contains spaces or special keys, you should surround the entire string with double quotation marks.

INITIAL SCRIPT

When you boot-up an MS-DOS computer, the first command that is executed is the AUTOEXEC.BAT file, if it exists. Under UNIX, every time you log in, a similar file (called the log-in script) is executed. The name of the log-in script is **.profile** for the Bourne and Korn shells and **.login** for the C shell.

The contents of the log-in script depend on how your administrator has initially set it up as well as any changes to it that you make. In Chapter 4, we edit this script.

Workout Shell variables and log-in script

---

1. Print out the values of the environment variables.

```
$ printenv
$ export     (Bourne shell—some versions)
```

2. Set your own environment variable.

```
$ MY-NAME="some-value"     (Bourne, Korn shells)
$ export MY-NAME

$ setenv MY-NAME "some-value"     (C shell)
```

3. Type

```
$ echo $MY-NAME
```

The output will be a line with the current value of MY-NAME. "$" precedes the name of an environment variable when you want the shell to replace it with the value of the variable.

4. Type out the log-in script.

```
$ more .profile     (Korn, Bourne shells)
$ more .login     (C shell)
```

You will probably see a line that sets **PATH** or **path**, and other lines that execute **stty** or other programs.

INPUT/OUTPUT REDIRECTION

Like MS-DOS, UNIX supports input and output redirection and pipes. In fact, MS-DOS borrowed the idea of redirection from UNIX. The output of many commands goes to the standard output, which is usually the terminal screen. To redirect the output, use the > character followed by a filename. For example,

```
$ ls > your-file
```

redirects the output of the `ls` command to a file called **your-file**. If the file already exists, it will be overwritten. C shell and Korn shell users have a **noclobber** feature, which is turned on by typing **set noclobber**. If the file exists and **noclobber** is on, the output file will not be overwritten.

You can append output to a file using **>>** followed by a filename. For example,

```
ls >> your-file
```

appends the output from `ls` to the existing file **your-file**. If **your-file** did not exist, it would be created.

To combine a number of files into a single file, you can use either the **cat** command with multiple filenames or the append operation. For example,

```
cat one.doc two.doc three.doc > combined.doc
```

and

```
cat one.doc > combined.doc
cat two.doc >> combined.doc
cat three.doc >> combined.doc
```

both produce **combined.doc**, which contains a copy of each of the three files.

Redirecting input for programs that read from the standard input (keyboard) causes the program to read from the specified file. The input direction character is <. The **cat** command reads from the standard input if no files are specified on the command line, and writes to the standard output. So

```
cat < one.doc
```

reads **one.doc** and outputs it to the screen. The line

```
cat < one.doc > one.copy
```

reads **one.doc** and outputs it to **one.copy**.

There is a special file named **/dev/null**. If you redirect input from this file, the input will terminate immediately. For example, if you typed

```
cat < /dev/null > temp
```

temp will be created with nothing in it. This has the same effect as if you typed

```
$ cat > temp
<control-D>
```

Unlike MS-DOS, UNIX handles zero-length files no differently than it handles other files.

As with MS-DOS, the pipe takes the output of one command and inputs that to another command. You type both commands on the same line, separated with a **|**, as

command parameters **|** *command parameters*

For example,

```
$ cat presidents | more
```

passes the output of the **cat** command (which is the contents of **presidents**) to the input of **more**. You need to have at least 25 lines in **presidents** to see any difference between the result of this command and that of **cat presidents** all by itself.

FILENAMES AND THE SHELL

As described in Chapter 2, the shell expands sets of characters that contain wildcard characters (***** and **?**) to matching filenames. There are other characters that are used by the shell for particular purposes, which are described in Chapter 8. These are '%', ';', '|', '*', '?', '␣', '`', '\\', '?', '[', ']', '(', ')', '$', '<', '>', '{','}', '^', and '#'. You should not use any of these characters in filenames or you may have a difficult time in listing or manipulating the files. In addition, the shell uses '-' for particular purposes, so you should not use it as the first character of a filename. If you preface one of these special characters with the escape character ('\\'), it is no longer treated as a special character by the shell. You may also put special characters inside quotation marks to prevent the shell from interpreting them.

One example will point out a situation you can get yourself into by using these special characters. Suppose that you entered

```
$ cat > "*"
```

This creates a file named *. If you enter **ls** *, you get a list of all the files, which includes the file *. If you type **ls** "*", you get a listing of just the * file. If you attempted to remove this file by typing **rm** *, all the files in the current directory would be removed. You need to use **rm** "*" to remove just the file named *.

LOGGING OFF

How you log off the system depends on the shell. You end input to the Bourne or the Korn shell with <control-D>. With the C shell, you type **logout**. You may also use <control-D> with the C shell if your log-in script does not contain **set ignoreeof**.

ERROR MESSAGES

You may get an error message reported back from the shell or from a program. The messages are short and use common phrases and syntax, such as

```
name: error-string
```

where *name* is a filename or other identifier and *error-string* is an entry listed in Table 3-1. This table gives only the most common messages. Since the same *error-string* is used by many programs, it is sometimes difficult to determine exactly what the real cause of the error may be. You can use **manerrno** to get further information on the potential causes of these messages.

TABLE 3-1 Error Messages for Files and Directories

ERROR MESSAGE	COMMON CAUSE
No such file or directory	You tried to list a file that does not exist or to change to a directory that does not exist.
Not a directory	You attempted to change the directory to a name that exists but which is not a directory.
Permission denied	You do not have the necessary permission for a file (read, write, or execute).
No space left on device	The disk is full.

FOR FURTHER INFORMATION

Bolsky, Morris I. 1986. *The UNIX System User's Handbook.* Englewood Cliffs, N.J.: Prentice Hall.

COMMAND SUMMARY

Setting environment variables	`name=value` and
	export `name` (sh, ksh)
	setenv `name value` (csh)
Printing environment variables	**printenv**
	export (some sh)
Login scripts	**.profile** (sh, ksh)
	.login (csh)
Input, output redirection	
Output	**>**
Output with append	**>>**
Input	**<**
Printing terminal keys	**stty**
Setting terminal characters	**stty** `key-name new-character`
Erase previous character	**erase** `character`
Erase entire line key	**kill** `character`
Interrupt key	**intr** `character`
Quit key	**quit** `character`
Stop output	**stop** `character`
Restart output	**start** `character`

4 | A COMMON EDITOR: VI

Better than a typewriter

You may wish to skip this chapter if your system has another editor installed, such as WordPerfect. However, **vi** is found on practically all UNIX systems, so it is handy to know a little bit about it. Your system may also have the **emacs** editor, which is described in Chapter 5.

EDITORS

MS-DOS provides a line-oriented editor called EDLIN. Many users use EDLIN only in an emergency. MS-DOS 5.0 supplies a full-screen editor that has some standard word-processing features. UNIX has both a line-oriented editor (**ed**) and a full screen editor (**vi**). The **ed** program uses commands similar to EDLIN. The full screen editor **vi** is easier to work with. By the way **vi** stands for the visual mode of the **ex** editor.

The commands in most editors allow you to do a number of common operations: open a file; save a file; move through a file; copy, move, and delete a block of text; find text; and find and replace text. These operations and a few other **vi** commands for performing basic text-editing operations are described here. You should note that **vi** is a text editor, not a word processor. Formatted output with page headers, different fonts, and other style is performed by **nroff** and **troff** (described in Chapter 13).

There are many versions of **vi**. The version described is a basic one. Your version may be more advanced and have features such as the ability to move the cursor without exiting input mode.

COMMAND AND INPUT MODES

vi has two modes, command and input. While in command mode, characters you type are interpreted as commands. Almost every character is recognized as a command, with different operations for upper- and lower-case letters. If you have difficulty entering commands, you should check the caps lock on your terminal to see if you are entering commands in the wrong case.

If the character you enter while in command mode is **:**, the program goes into "last-line" mode. The characters you type after the ":" appear at the bottom of the screen. The string is interpreted as a command when you press the <Return> key. You can edit the command prior to pressing <Return>. The origin of last-line commands comes from the **ed** program. You will see that there are sometimes two ways to execute the same operation: a command mode character and a last-line command.

In input mode, every character you type until you hit the <Escape> character is added to the text buffer. The program enters input mode for certain commands, such as **i**.

Some versions of **vi** allow you to move around the text buffer with the cursor keys while you are in input mode. Other versions do not. A common error is to use the cursor keys while in input mode in these versions. Extra characters appear on the screen. Be sure to terminate input mode with <Escape> before attempting any commands.

This distinction of modes is not common with MS-DOS text processors. On MS-DOS programs, keys in conjunction with the Control or Alt key or function keys are typically used for commands. A character by itself is added to the text buffer.

COMMANDS

vi has a large number of commands for moving around in a file and for deleting and changing text. The basic commands are covered here. The remainder are listed in the **man** pages for **vi**. Many commands can be prefaced with a count. For example, **x** deletes a single character and **10x** deletes 10 characters. If no count is specified, the default is 1. Some commands that differ only by case are related. For example, **x** deletes the character the cursor is on, and **X** deletes the character to the left of the cursor.

Opening and Saving a File

To open a file, type **vi** *filename*. If the file is new, the screen is filled with lines with a '~' in column 1. The cursor is in the upper left corner. If the file currently exists, its contents appear on the screen. Lines after the end of the file appear with a '~' in column 1.

Like many MS-DOS word processors, any changes you make to the text are not saved to the disk file unless you explicitly perform a save operation. To save the file by writing it to disk, type **:w<Return>**. To quit the **vi** program, type **:q<Return>**. You may combine the save and quit operations with **:wq** or **ZZ**. If you want to quit **vi** without saving any of your changes, type **:q!**. To save a file, you must have write permission for an existing file or write permission for the directory of a new file.

You should be aware that like many common word processors **vi** does not make a backup file. If you want to keep a backup, you should copy the file before editing it. Writing a shell script that includes making a backup copy is discussed in Chapters 10 and 11.

Moving the Cursor

The arrow keys move the cursor up and down a line and left and right a character. The **k**, **j**, **h**, and **l** keys are alternatives for these same actions. The **$** and **^** keys move the cursor to the beginning and end of a line. As we will see in Chapter 9, those keys are used by a number of programs to represent the start and end of a line. The **H** and **L** keys move to the top and bottom of the screen. To go forward and backward a screen, use **<control-F>** and **<control-B>**. If you want to go to a particular line number, type the number followed by **G** and the cursor will be positioned on that line.

Inserting Text

To enter input mode, type **i**. The characters you type are entered into the text buffer. Depending on your version of **vi**, you may be able to use the cursor keys to reposition the cursor while remaining in input mode. If you type a cursor key and garbage characters appear, you do not have that feature. You exit from input mode with <Escape>. [1] With **i**, the input text goes before the cursor position. You can start input after the cursor with **a**. The **I** and **A** commands start input at the beginning and end of the current line. While in insert mode, you can use the <backspace> key to delete the current character.

---

[1] On some machines, the function key F11 is the <escape> key.

Overwriting Text

To overwrite the single character at the cursor, type **r** followed by the new character. To overwrite a string of characters, type **R**, followed by the new characters. End overwriting with <Escape>.

Deleting Text

To delete a single character, position the cursor over the character and type **x**. To delete a word, move the cursor to the first character of the word and type **dw**. If the cursor is on a character within the word, only that character and ones following it in the word will be deleted. A word stops at the next space or punctuation mark.

Deleting, Moving, and Copying Text Blocks

vi uses an internal paste buffer concept. If you delete or copy some text, the set of characters goes into the paste buffer. You can position the cursor to a location and paste the contents of the paste buffer into the text at that location. To delete a line of text, use **dd**. To delete a number of lines, type the number followed by **dd**. The mnemonic synonym for copying is yanking. To copy a line of text into the paste buffer, type **yy**. To copy a number of lines, type the number followed by **yy**. To paste the contents of the buffer after the current cursor position, use **p**. To paste the contents to the left of the cursor, use **P**. On some versions, if you perform other editing commands after the delete or copy, the paste buffer becomes invalid.

Searching and Replacing Text

You search for text with the **/** command, as

```
/pattern <Return>
```

The screen is moved so that the line containing a match to the *pattern* will be visible on the screen. The *pattern* can be a text string or a regular expression, which is described in Chapter 9. For example,

```
/Adams <Return>
```

will position the screen so that the next line containing the string "Adams" is visible. To search again, type **/** **<Return>**.

You can replace a string with another string with **:s**, as in

```
:start-line,end-lines/pattern/substitution/
```

The substitution is made only on the current line unless you specify a range of lines. To make the substitution on all lines in the file, use **1,$**. The **$** symbol represents the last line in the file. The substitution will be made only once per line unless you specify **g** after the final **/**. For example,

```
:s/Sam/Bill/
```

changes **Sam** to **Bill** on the current line;

```
:1,$s/Sam/Bill/g
```

changes **Sam** to **Bill** everywhere in the file.[2]

Miscellaneous Commands

You can read another file into the text buffer by typing **:r** followed by the filename. You must have read permission for the file. If you want to spawn another shell (similar to escaping to DOS from many commercial programs), type **:!**. Line numbering can be turned on and off with **:set number** and **:set nonumber**. The line numbers are not stored in the file, just displayed on the screen. Another useful command that redraws the screen is **<control-l>**. This might be needed if you are communicating with the UNIX system via a phone line and erroneous characters are received that mess up your display.

The undo command (**u**) undoes the last editing change. If you accidentally type the wrong command, **u** will undo whatever operation that command performed. The undo command has only a one-step history. If you type **u** again, it will undo the last command (which was **u**).

---

[2] You can also have more complex replacement strings. These are shown in the description of **sed** in Chapter 9.

Workout vi

In one of the first workouts, you created a file called **presidents**. Unless you were a perfect typist, you probably made some mistakes. You can now use **vi** to correct the file. If you did not create the file, you can do so now.

If **vi** does not work properly (by putting garbage characters on the screen or characters in the wrong place), the **TERM** environment variable may be set improperly. Exit **vi** by typing **:q!**. Determine your terminal type name, such as "VT100" (or ask the system administrator). Then type either

```
$ TERM=terminal-type-name (Bourne, Korn)
$ export TERM
```

or

```
$ setenv TERM terminal-type-name (C Shell)
```

Then restart **vi**.

1. Start **vi** and edit **presidents**.

   ```
   $ vi presidents
   ```

   If you previously created **presidents**, you will see the lines on the screen. If not, every line will have a ~ in column 1.
2. Move the cursor to the end of the file. Hit the <down arrow> or **j** key enough times to move to the end.
3. Type **A** to start input at the end of the last line. If you do not have anything in the file, start entering the **presidents**, as shown in the Workout on page 7. If you already have text in the file, add the last few presidents:

   ```
   31 Hoover Herbert Clark
   32 Roosevelt Franklin Delano
   33 Truman Harry S
   34 Eisenhower Dwight David
   35 Kennedy John Fitzgerald
   36 Johnson Lyndon Baines
   37 Nixon Richard Milhous
   38 Ford Gerald Rudolph
   39 Carter James Earl
   40 Reagan Ronald Wilson
   41 Bush George H.
   42 Clinton William Jefferson
   ```

   When you are done with the input, type <Escape>.
4. Now go back to the beginning of the file, using the <up arrow> or **k**, or **1G**. Check each line for proper spelling and that the number is separated by a space from the first name and a space separates the last name from the first name.

5. If you made an error in the order of the input, such as typing "40 Reagan Ronald" before "1 Washington George", use delete and paste. Position the cursor on the line to move.
   Type **dd**.
   Position the cursor anywhere on the line where the text should be inserted.
   Type **p**.
6. Go back to the beginning with **1G**. Then search for "J" with

   `/J <return>`

   Try it several times to see how the screen is positioned.
7. When you are satisfied with the text, save and exit by typing

   `:wq`

Workout Initial log-in program

1. Edit your initial log-in program.

   ```
   $ vi .profile     (sh, ksh)
   $ vi .login       (csh)
   ```

2. Make any changes you would like, such as using **stty** to alter the input keys (see page 30).
3. Save the file. Then execute it with

   ```
   $ . .profile      (sh, ksh)
   $ source .login   (csh)
   ```

   Notice the differences in the changes you made.

FOR FUTHER INFORMATION

Bell Labs, Bolsky, M. I. 1988. *The Vi User's Handbook.* Englewood Cliffs, N.J.: Prentice Hall.

El, L. M. 1985. *Editing in a UNIX Environment: The Vi-ex Editor.* Englewood Cliffs, N.J.: Prentice Hall.

Hewlett-Packard, 1989. *The Ultimate Guide to the vi and ex Text Editors.* Addison-Wesley.

Lamb, L. 1987. *Learning the Vi Editor.* Sebastopol, Calif: O'Reilly and Associates.

Sonnenschein, Dan. 1987. *A Guide to Vi: Visual Editing on the UNIX System.* Englewood Cliffs, N.J.: Prentice Hall.

COMMAND SUMMARY

Starting up	**vi** *filename(s)*
Saving files	
Save buffer to disk	**:w** or **ZZ**
Save buffer to named file	**:w** *filename*
Save and quit	**:wq**
Quit without saving	**:q!**
Save buffer to disk and open next file	**:n**
Moving around	
Up a line	**k** or \<up arrow\>
Down a line	**j** or \<down arrow\>
Left a character	**h** or \<left arrow\>
Right a character	**l** or \<right arrow\>
Beginning of line	**$**
End of line	**^**
Top of screen	**H**
Bottom of screen	**L**
Forward a screen	**\<control-F\>**
Backward a screen	**\<control-B\>**
Go to a line number	*number***G**
Input	
Insert text before cursor	**i**
Append text after cursor	**a**
Insert text at beginning of current line	**I**
Append text after current line	**A**
Escape from input mode	\<Escape\>

Overwriting text
    Replace single character   **r**
        Replace string of characters   **R**
        End overwriting a string   \<Escape\>
    Deleting text (deleted text goes to internal buffer)
        Delete character at cursor   **x**
        Delete word   **dw**
        Delete current line   **dd**
        Delete number of lines   *number***dd**
    Copying text (to internal buffer)
        Copying (yanking) single line   **yy**
        Copying (yanking) number of lines   *number***yy**
    Pasting deleted or copied text (from internal buffer)
        Paste text after cursor   **p**
        Paste text before cursor   **P**
    Searching and replacing
        Searching   **/***pattern*
        Replacing   **:***start-line, end-line***s** **/***pattern/substitution/*
    Miscellaneous
        Read a file from disk into buffer   **:r** *filename*
        Spawn a UNIX shell   **:!**
        Turn numbering on and off   **:set number**
                                       :set nonumber
        Redraw the screen   **\<control-1\>**
        Undo last edit command   **u**

5 | ANOTHER EDITOR: EMACS

A choice rather than an echo

The **emacs** editor is present on many UNIX systems. It is a powerful, configurable editor. The source code is available from Richard Stallman's Free Software Foundation, so you could compile and run it on your system if it is not currently available. The BRIEF editor on MS-DOS is similar to **emacs**.

EDITORS

The commands in most editors allow you to do a number of operations: Open a file; Save a File; Cursor through a file; Copy, Move, and Delete a block of text; Find text; and Find/replace text. These operations and a few other **emacs** commands for performing basic text editing operations are described here. You should note that **emacs** is a text editor, not a word processor. Formatted output with page headers, different fonts, and other style is performed by **nroff** and **troff** (described in Chapter 13).

There are many versions of **emacs**. Your version may be set up with different keys. The help commands will lead you through appropriate information.

Help

There are a number of different help options that are reached via
`<control-h>`. One is `<control-h> a` for showing commands that match
a string. For example, if you enter

    file

you will get a list of function names that include the word `file`. To see
what key performs a particular function, use `<control-h> w`. For example, to find out which key turns on or off **overwrite-mode**, enter

    <control-h> w

and then in response to the prompt, enter

    overwrite-mode

The function names are listed in the command summary. To see which
function a particular key runs, use `<control-h> c` and then type the key
you want to know about. On many systems, there is an **emacs** tutorial that
is reached via `<control-h> t`. Follow the instructions that are listed in it.

Windows and Buffers

There are multiple windows in **emacs**. Each window can be displaying a portion of the same text buffer or a different text buffer. To keep
things simple in the beginning, use only a single window to edit text. If you
ask for help, it appears in a separate window. You can switch back and
forth between the text and the help window with `<control-X> o`. To
delete the help window, when the cursor is in help window, use
`<control-X> 0`. When the cursor is in the window of the text you are
editing, use `<control-X> 1`. Control keys are listed in the documentation
as "C - X", where X is the letter of the key and the <Esc> is listed as "M".

In response to some commands, you may see other buffers appear in
your editing window. To list the buffers, use `<control-x><control-b>`.
To get the window back to a particular file, find the file on the list. Then
use `<control-x> b` and specify that file.

COMMANDS

emacs works much like MS-DOS word processors with which you may be
familiar. The normal keys that you type are entered into the text buffer.

Control keys (e.g., `<control-b>`) perform commands. The commands consist of a set of single-keystroke commands and two sets of multiple-keystroke commands. The multiple-keystroke functions generally begin with one of two characters: `<control-X>` and `<Esc>`. If a command requires arguments, such as a file to write to, it will prompt you for the values.

Every command in **emacs** has a name associated with it. For example, the name for moving one character to the left is "forward-char". Commands are usually associated with a set of keystrokes. The set of keystrokes which are shown in this chapter are the most common default associations. You can set up your own keystrokes to command relationships.

If a command does not have keystrokes associated with it, you can use:

`<Esc> x` *name-of-command*

Listed in the summary at the end of the chapter are the names of the commands and their typical keystrokes. For example, if "overwrite-mode" does not have a set of keystrokes, as shown by the help screen, you can use

`<Esc> x overwrite-mode`

Opening and Saving a File

To open a file, type **emacs** *filename*. If the file is new, a blank window will appear. If the file currently exists, its contents appear on the screen. To save the file (write it back to the disk), type `<control-X><control-S>`. To quit the **emacs** program, type `<control-X><control-C>`. Unless you explicitly save a file, the changes will not be written to disk. You must have permission to write to the file, or in the case of a new file, to the directory. If you try to quit without saving a changed file, **emacs** will prompt you with a question as to whether or not you want to save the file.

It should be noted that **emacs** does not make a backup file, like many common word processors. If you want to keep a backup, you should copy the file before editing it. How to write a shell script to do this is described in Chapter 8.

Moving Around in a File

On most versions, the arrow keys move the cursor up and down a line, and left and right a character. The `<control-p>`, `<control-n>`, `<control-b>`, and `<control-f>` keys perform the same operations. The `<control-a>` and `<control-e>` keys move the cursor to the beginning and end of a line. To go forward and backward a screen, use `<control-v>`

and `<Esc> v`. To go to the beginning or end of a buffer, use `<Esc> <` and `<Esc> >`. If you want to go to a particular line, you use the "goto-line" command. The default keystrokes for this vary, but you can use `<Esc> x goto-line`.

Inserting Text

The characters you type, other than commands, will be entered into the text buffer. To switch to overwrite mode, use the appropriate command, as found by the help sequence mentioned in the help section or use `<Esc> x overwrite-mode`.

Deleting Text

To delete a single character, position the cursor over the character and type `control-d>`. There are many other commands for deleting partial sets of text, such as words, everything to the end of the line, and so on. These are listed in the help for `emacs`. `emacs` distinguishes between deleting text, which is irrecoverable, and killing text, which deletes it from the current location and places it in a paste buffer.

Deleting, Moving, and Copying Text Blocks

`emacs` uses the internal paste buffer concept. If you kill a set of text, it goes into the paste buffer. You can position the cursor and then paste the contents of that buffer into the text. To kill a line of text, starting at the cursor position, use `<control-k>`. To kill a block of text, mark the beginning of the text with `<control-@>`. Move the cursor to the other end of the text and type `<control-w>`.

A mnemonic synonym for copying is yanking. The contents of the paste buffer is yanked (copied) after the current cursor position with `<control-y>`.

Searching and Replacing Text

You search for text with `<control-s>`. The command will ask for a string to search for. The screen will be moved so that the cursor will be on the matching string. This search is an incremental search. Enter `<Esc>` when you have completed the string to search for or `<control-s>` to search for the next occurrence. You can search for regular expressions, which are described in Chapter 9, using `<Esc><control-S>`. The `<control-g>` command aborts a search.

`<Esc> %` is used to replace a string with another string. This command asks for an old string and a new string. If it finds the old string, it asks if you want to replace it, if you want to quit, or if you want to replace all remaining instances in the file. Replace the string and go to the next occurrence with `<space>`, skip the replacement and go to the next match with **n**, replace all remaining occurrences with **!**, and quit with `<control-g>`.

Miscellaneous Commands

To write the current text to a file, use `<control-x><control-w>`. If you want to spawn another shell (similar to escaping to DOS from many commercial programs), type `<Esc> x shell`. Another useful command redraws the screen `<control-l>`. This may be needed if you are communicating with the UNIX system via a phone line and erroneous characters are received. You can undo an editing command with `<control-x> u`.

You can specify that a command be run many times by prefacing it with `<control-u>`, followed by a number. The next command you type will be run that many times. For example, to delete eight letters, use

```
<control-u>8<control-d>
```

Workout emacs

In one of the first workouts, you created a file called **presidents**. Unless you were a perfect typist, you probably made some mistakes. You can now use **emacs** to correct the file. If you did not create the file, you can do so now.

If **emacs** does not work properly (by putting garbage characters on the screen or characters in the wrong place, the **TERM** environment variable may be set improperly. Exit **emacs** by typing `<control-x> <control-c>`. Determine your terminal type name, such as "VT100" (or ask the system administrator). Then type either

```
$ TERM=terminal-type-name   (Bourne, Korn shells)
$ export TERM
```

or

```
$ setenv TERM terminal-type-name   (C shell)
```

Then restart **emacs**.

1. Start **emacs** and edit `presidents`.

   ```
   $ emacs presidents
   ```

2. Move the cursor to the end of the file. Hit the `<down arrow>` or `<control-n>` keys to move to the end, or use `<Esc>` `>`.

3. If you do not have anything in the file, start entering the `presidents`, as shown in the Workout on page 7. If you already have text in the file, add the last few presidents:

   ```
   31 Hoover Herbert Clark
   32 Roosevelt Franklin Delano
   33 Truman Harry S
   34 Eisenhower Dwight David
   35 Kennedy John Fitzgerald
   36 Johnson Lyndon Baines
   37 Nixon Richard Milhous
   38 Ford Gerald Rudolph
   39 Carter James Earl
   40 Reagan Ronald Wilson
   41 Bush George H.
   42 Clinton William Jefferson
   ```

4. Now go back to the beginning of the file, using the `<up arrow>` , `<control-p>`, or `<Esc>` `<`. Check each line for proper spelling and that the number is separated by space from the first name and a space separates the last name from the first name.

5. If you made an error in the order of the input, such as typing "40 Reagan Ronald" before "1 Washington George", use delete and paste. Position the cursor on the first character of the line to move. Type

   ```
   <control-k>
   ```

   Delete the blank line with

   ```
   <control-d>
   ```

   Position the cursor at the end of the line where the text should be inserted. Type

   ```
   <Return>
   <control-y>
   ```

The `<Return>` makes a blank line in which to put the yanked text. Alternatively, you could use `<control-@>` and `<control-w>` to mark and kill the line.

6. When you are satisfied with the text, save and exit by typing

```
<control-x><control-s>
<control-x><control-c>
```

Workout Initial log-in program

1. Edit your initial log-in program.

```
$ emacs .profile      (sh, ksh)
$ emacs .login        (csh)
```

2. Make any changes you would like, such as using **stty** to alter the input keys.
3. Save the file. Then execute it with

```
$ . .profile          (sh, ksh)
$ source .login       (csh)
```

Notice the differences in the changes you made.

FOR FURTHER INFORMATION

You will want to try out multiple windows and multiple buffers. You can change the key bindings, so that you can use your favorite keys to perform the standard editing operations. You can write macros so that a few keystrokes will perform a number of operations. Check the **emacs** tutorial on your system.

Stallman, Richard. 1991. *GNU EMACS Manual.* Free Software Foundation.

Cameron, Debra, and Bill Rosenblatt. 1992. *Learning GNU Emacs.* O'Reilly.

Schoonover, J. Bowie, and W. Arnold. 1992. *GNU Emacs Unix Text Editing and Programming.* Addison-Wesley.

COMMAND SUMMARY

Starting up	**emacs** *filename*
Saving files	
Save buffer to disk save-buffer	`<control-x><control-s>`
Save buffer to named file write-file	`<control-x><control-w>`
Quit save-buffers-kill-emacs	`<control-x><control-c>`
Moving around	
Up a line previous-line	`<control-p>` or \<up arrow\>
Down a line next-line	`<control-n>` or \<down arrow\>
Left a character backward-char	`<control-b>` or \<left arrow\>
Right a character forward-char	`<control-f>` or \<right arrow\>
Beginning of line beginning-of-line	`<control-a>`
End of line end-of-line	`<control-e>`
Forward a screen scroll-up	`<control-v>`
Backward a screen scroll-down	`<Esc> v`
Beginning of buffer beginning-of-buffer	`<Esc> <`
End of buffer end-of-buffer	`<Esc> >`
Deleting text	
Delete current character delete-char	`<control-d>`
Killing text (to internal buffer)	
Kill remainder of line from cursor kill-line	`<control-k>`

Mark beginning of block	`<control-@>`
set-mark-command	
Kill from mark to cursor	`<control-w>`
kill-region	
Yanking text (from internal buffer)	
Paste text before cursor	`<control-y>`
yank	
Searching and replacing	
Search for string	`<control-s>`
isearch-forward	
Search for pattern	`<Esc><control-S>`
isearch-forward-regexp	
Quit search	`<control-g>`
abort-recursive-edit	
Replacing	`<Esc> %`
query-replace	
Miscellaneous	
Spawn a UNIX shell	`<Esc> x shell`
shell	
Redraw the screen	`<control-l>`
recenter	
Undo editing command	`<control-x> u`
advertised-undo	
Running a function	`<Esc> x` *name-of-function*
execute-extended-command	
Multiple command executions	`<control-u>`*number command*
universal-argument	
Help	
Commands that match	`<control-h> a`
command-apropos	
Functions for key	`<control-h> c`
describe-key-briefly	
Key for function	`<control-h> w`
where-is	
Tutorial	`<control-h> t`
help-with-tutorial	
Windows and buffers	
Switching between two windows	`<control-X> o`
Delete help window	`<control-X> 0` or `<control-X> 1`
Listing buffers	`<control-x><control-b>`
Selecting another buffer	`<control-x> b`

6 | OTHER USERS

You're not alone

You may not be the only user on your UNIX system. Unlike MS-DOS, UNIX was designed as a multiuser operating system. You can communicate with the other users via a chat mode or mail or by sharing files. UNIX also has the concept of a group, which is a set of users sharing a common set of files.

GROUPS

Groups are a way of sharing files with a set of other users. You are automatically a member of at least one group, usually named something like **usr** or **other**. Every file has two owners: an individual user and a group. The permissions for each file include user permissions and group permissions. If the group permissions for a file allow reading, writing, or executing, any other user who is a member of the group owning that file can perform those operations. The system administrator creates groups and add users to groups.

You can be a member of more than one group. The two versions of UNIX differ in how your membership in multiple groups works. In BSD, you are a member of multiple groups simultaneously. If you belong to the group that owns the file, you are granted the group permissions. If you create a file, its group owner is made the same as the group that owns the directory in which it is created. You must have write privileges for that directory.

With System V, you belong to a single group at a time. When you attempt to access a file, group permissions are checked only for that current group. If you create a file, its group ownership is your current group. To change groups, you use the **newgrp** command. Its syntax is

newgrp *group*

PERMISSIONS

When UNIX checks permissions for access to a file, it first checks to see if you are the owner of the file. If so, the user permissions are checked. If you are not the owner, your current group or groups (depending on the version of UNIX) are matched against the group owner of the file. If there is a match, the group permissions are checked. If neither of these cases apply, the world (other) permissions are checked. The world is considered to be all the remaining users on a particular system.

To change the permissions for any of the three categories, you use **chmod**, as introduced in Chapter 2. Its syntax is

chmod *permissions filename*

The permissions are in the form [**ugo**][**+-**][**rwx**]. You select **u** for a user who is the owner (i.e., you), **g** for group, or **o** for other, followed by **+** to add permissions or **-** to subtract permissions, and **r** for read permission, **w** for write permission, or **x** for execute permission. For example,

chmod g+r presidents

gives read permission to users in the group that owns **presidents**. You can also specify permissions with an = symbol. For example,

chmod u=rw one.doc

sets read and write permissions for you on **one.doc**.

Permissions for directories have different meanings than for regular files. If you have read permission for a directory, the names of the files in it can be read (e.g., for listing directories with **ls**). If you do not have read permission, the names cannot be read, so to use a particular file, you will have to know that it exists. If you have execute permission for a directory, that directory can be searched for a particular file (e.g., in looking for a pathname). If you do not, you cannot use the files in the directory or any of its subdirectories.

The Permission Mask

There is a file creation mask that is applied to the permissions of every file that you create. This mask is called the **umask**. The mask has three octal digits. Each digit represents the permissions for the user, group, and other. The values for each digit are 4 for read, 2 for write, and 1 for execute. For example, 421 means user read, group write, and other execute permissions. The value 700 is interpreted as user read/write/execute and no permissions for group and other.

You specify with **umask** the permissions you do *not* want a created file to have. This mask is applied to files which are subsequently created by programs or by I/O redirection. For example,

```
umask 077
```

will turn off read, write, and execute permissions for group and others for all files that are created after the mask is executed.

Diagram of **umask** example

	User			Group			Other		
	r	w	x	r	w	x	r	w	x
umask 077	0	0	0	1	1	1	1	1	1
Permission mask on created files	1	1	1	0	0	0	0	0	0

CHANGING OWNERS

You may wish to transfer ownership of a file to another user or another group. You could let the other user make a copy of your file and then erase your copy. Alternatively, you can use the change owner (**chown**) and change group (**chgrp**) commands to change ownership. The syntax is

```
chown new-owner filename(s)
```

and

```
chgrp new-group filename(s)
```

On some systems, only the system administrator is able to change the ownership of files.

THE OTHER USERS

You may want to find out the ids of the other users on your system. A list of all users who are set up on a system is kept in the file **/etc/passwd**. This file is owned by the system administrator, but all users usually have read permission. To see the file, you can use **cat** or **more**. The file contains a number of lines, one per user, each broken into a number of fields which are separated by semicolons. The fields include the user log-in name, the initial group, the user password (which is encoded), the user number, the shell that will be started at log-in, and a comment field.

To find out which users are currently logged onto the system, you can use **who**. This lists the user's name, terminal, and log-in time for each current user. If you just want to find out this information about yourself, type

```
who am i
```

Chatting with Other Users

You can write an immediate message to a user by using the **write** command. The message appears on the user's screen unless he/she has turned the ability off by executing **mesg n**. The command is:

write *user-name*

Everything you type until you hit <control-D> will appear on your screen and the other user's screen.

The other user may write back to you before you have finished. Your lines and his/her lines will get intermixed. To avoid this situation, a convention has been established, similar to radio. You type 'o' on a single line to say that your current thought is "over". The other user then responds and finishes his/her thoughts with an 'o'. Just before you end your entire communication, type 'oo' for over and out.

If you do not wish to be interrupted with writes from other users, type **mesg n**. To reset this ability, type **mesg y**.

You can also interactively communicate with other users using **talk**, as

talk *user-name*

If the other user responds with **talk** *your-user-name*, communication is established. A screen appears, split into two parts. What you type appears in one part, what the other user types appears in the other part. You end **talk** with <control-C>.

MAIL

You can mail a message to any other user on your system. If your computer is interconnected to other computers, you can mail a message to a user on one of those computers. If your system is connected to a worldwide network such as the Internet or is a part of Usenet, you can send a message to almost anyone who has access to electronic mail.

The basic program for sending and receiving mail is **mail**. System V users can use **mailx**. Other mail programs may be available on local system—check with your system administrator. Basic operation of all the programs is the same. The additional features make it easier to set up distribution lists, copy mail into mail to be sent, and so on.

To send someone mail, you execute **mail** *user-name*. The **mail** program takes your input as a message to send to *user-name*. Depending on the version of mail, it may ask for a subject. Once you start typing, everything goes into the message until you type <control-D> or a line that contains just a period. If you change your mind about sending the message, type <control-C> to quit **mail**. To send the same message to multiple users, list all the ids on the command line, such as

```
mail user-name1 user-name2
```

The mail message is routed to its destination by other mail-related programs. Each user on a UNIX system has a file called a mailbox. This file is typically named **/usr/spool/mail/***user-name* or **/usr/mail/***user-name*. The environment variable MAIL has the name of your file. When a message is received by this user, it is appended to the end of this file.

To read your mail, just type **mail**. The program reads your mailbox and displays the messages in your mailbox. Some versions give a list of the subjects and senders of all the messages and permit you to choose which message to read. Others print them sequentially, using either last-in or first-in order.

After displaying a message, **mail** prompts you with **?** for what to do with the message. You can delete it with **d**. If you do not delete it, it remains in your mailbox. You go onto the next message with <Return> or **+**. You can go back a message with **-** or reprint the current message with **p**. With some versions you can type a number and the corresponding message in the mailbox will appear. To quit the program, type **q**. Messages that you have deleted will be removed from your mailbox. If you quit the program with **x**, deleted messages will not be removed from the mailbox.

You can save a copy of a message in another file. Messages contain both the contents and a header, which shows the route via which the message was transmitted. To save the entire message, at the **?** prompt, enter **s**. This saves the message in a file named **mbox**. To save it in another file, enter **s** *filename*. To save just the contents of the message, use **w** or **w** *filename*. You can mail the message to someone else with **m** *user name*.

Network Connections

If your system is connected to a network, you can send mail to users on other systems. You need to know their mail address. The address will usually be one of two types. It may look like

```
user-name@something.something.something
```

or

```
system!system!system!user-name
```

The former is the Domain Name System style. This style is used for system names by the Internet, which is a worldwide network of computers. The computers on the Internet may be running any type of operating system. The latter style is a UUCP address, which stands for the UNIX-to-UNIX-CoPy program. [1]

Internet names are assigned on a global basis. Everything after the @ character designates a particular computer system.[2] Each string of characters separated by the periods has a meaning. The last string is designated the domain. For example, the domain "**com**" is used for commercial institutions and "**edu**" for educational institutions. The preceding string designates a particular institution, such as "dec" or "duke". Any preceding strings are particular to that institution. If the institution has more than one computer, it will add one or more strings to the name. For example, on one computer to which I have access, the string is **raphael.acpub. duke.edu**. This uniquely identifies a computer on the Internet.

The Internet is designed so that the name does not designate a particular routing. Your computer needs to know about a small number of other

---

[1] The mail routing program interprets each address and may convert the address from one of these styles to the other or even to an entirely different style.

[2] For those interested in details, an Internet name gets translated to a numeric Internet address, which is composed of four numbers, such as 52.21.18.93. This address designates a connection to a network rather than to a particular host computer.

computers with whom it can communicate directly.[3] If the mail address designates an unknown computer, the message is forwarded to a gateway computer. If the address is unknown to that computer, it is forwarded to that computer's gateway. The message may reach a backbone computer that knows the location of every Internet system and so can route the message to it via the appropriate system.

UUCP addresses specify a particular routing. The mail program sends the message to the first *system* listed. That system then forwards the message to the next *system* listed. When the message reaches the final system, it delivers it to the user. The way UUCP works is that one UNIX system calls up another UNIX system and delivers all the messages designated for it and receives any message for itself. The receiving system then calls up other UNIX systems and passes along messages that are designated for them. There are no central backbone computers and no gateways in the sense that the Internet uses them.[4]

You may see addresses that are a combination of the two styles, such as

```
system!system!user-name@something.something
```

This message can be sent to the Internet address that is specified (typically, it is "uunet.com") and then sent using UUCP via the path specified. Or it may be routed via UUCP and then sent onto the Internet by the last-named UNIX system. You may also see addresses such as

```
70125.1142@compuserve.com
```

The name of the user (`70125.1142`) is interpreted by the receiving system (`compuserve.com`).

If you are using the C shell with a UUCP address, you will need to use the shell escape character or put the address in quotes. For example,

```
mail xxxx!xxxx!xxxx
```

should be typed in the C shell as

```
mail xxxx\!xxxx\!xxxx
```

---

[3] A file lists the addresses of network connections known to a system.

[4] UUCP addresses can be changed by a smart mailer, based on a UUCP global database.

•

Workout `write` and `mail`

---

1. Find out who the other users are on your system.

   ```
   $ who
   ```

   You will get a list that includes lines containing

   ```
   user-name tty-id
   ```

2. If you personally know who one of the other users is, write a message to that user.

   ```
   $ write user-name
   Hi, I am just trying out the write command
   Would you write something back to me so I
   can see what it looks like.
   o
   ```

   Their response will appear on your screen. If they follow the convention, the last line will be an 'o'. Finish up by typing

   ```
   Thanks. Would you send me a mail message so
   I can try that out?
   Thanks.
   oo
   <control-D>
   ```

   You may see a response to this message, or the other user may just terminate `write`.

3. Mail yourself a message. Type

   ```
   $ mail your-user-name
   Subject: Test message
   This is a test message.
   I am sending to myself.
   <control-D>
   cc: <return>
   ```

You can use **mailx** if you are running on System V. Depending on your system, the "Subject" and the "cc" prompts may not come up.

4. Look at your mail. Type

```
$ mail
From: your-user-name
Subject: Test message
This is a test message.
I am sending to myself.
?
```

The first message you received is printed out and awaiting your disposition. Delete this message by typing

```
? d
```

Your mail program may print out a list of messages and subjects instead of just listing the first message. Select one by using the corresponding number.

If there are no more messages, the prompt will reappear. If not, the next message will be printed followed by the prompt. Delete that one also by typing **d**.

5. Quit the mail system.

```
? q
```

If you type **x** instead, the messages will be saved in your mailbox and you can try this workout again.

6. If your system is connected to the Internet, try sending a message to me:

```
$ mail Kpugh@allen.com
Subject: Workout
Trying out my workout
<control-D>
```

7. If another mail program is available on your system, try it out.

NEWS AND MESSAGES

Your system administrator may use the message or news system to keep you informed about the current state of the system. The programs **msgs** (BSD) or **news** (System V) display new system messages that have not yet been seen by the user. A call to one of these programs is usually part of your log-in script.

If you are connected to either the Internet or UUCP network, you may have Usenet available to you. This is an electronic bulletin board with a wide variety of business and personal topics. For example, the C language forum is **comp.lang.c** and the beer-making forum is **alt.beer**. There are a number of programs available for reading and responding to messages on the bulletin board, including **rnews, rn, trn**, and **nn**. Check with your system administrator to see which are available on your system.

NETWORKS

If you are connected to a network, you can log in to other computers on which you have accounts. You can also transfer files from another computer to your computer. The remote log-in (**rlogin**) program allows you to connect to other UNIX computers. The **telnet** program permits you to connect to non-UNIX computers. The remote copy (**rcp**) allows you to copy files to and from other UNIX computers. The file transfer program (**ftp**) permits transfer to and from non-UNIX computers.

These programs require the name of the remote computer and that you have some sort of permission to use the remote computer. Many computers have "guest" or "anonymous" accounts which allow you to receive files from them.

The syntax for the log-in programs consists of

    rlogin *hostname*

and

    telnet *hostname*

Once your log-in is accepted by the remote computer, you use the appropriate commands for that system. With **telnet** you can toggle between the remote computer and your local computer by using <control-]>. With **rlogin**, if you have job control, you can use ~<control-z> to switch to the local system.

The remote copy program has the syntax

```
rcp hostname:source-file destination-file
rcp source-file hostname:destination-file
```

The **rcp** program can also use directory names, just like **cp**. The remote system must be set up to recognize your system for this command to work. To use the file transfer program, the syntax is

```
ftp hostname
```

ftp has a number of commands, which are listed by entering **help** at the **ftp** prompt. The commands include:

Get file from remote host	**get** *file*
Get multiple files from remote host	**mget** *filename(s)*
Put file onto remote host	**put** *file*
Put multiple files onto remote host	**mput** *filename(s)*
Terminate connection with remote host	**bye**
List directory on remote host	**ls**
Change directory on remote host	**cd**
Select binary file transfer type	**binary**
Select ascii file transfer type	**ascii**

You may get an error message from any of these commands. The message usually reads "Host is down". The computer that you are attempting to contact is unable to respond. Either it may be down or the network may not be operating properly.

FOR FURTHER INFORMATION:

Anderson, Bart, Bryan Costales, and Harry Henderson. 1991. *The Waite Group's UNIX Communications*. Sams

Frey, Donnalyn, and Rick Adams. 1993. !%@:: *A Directory of Electronic Mail Addressing & Networks*. Sebastopol, Calif.: O'Reilly and Associates.

Kehoe, Brendan. 1992. *Zen and the Art of the Internet*. Englewood Cliffs, N.J.: Prentice Hall

Kochan, Stephen, and Patrick Wood (ed.). 1989. *UNIX Networking*. Hayden.

Krol, Ed. 1992. *The Whole Internet—User's Guide & Catalog*. O'Reilly.

Marine, A., S. Kirkpatrick, V. Leou, and C. Ward. 1992. *Internet: Getting Started*. Englewood Cliffs, N.J.: Prentice Hall.

O'Reilly, T., and Dougherty, D. 1987. *Managing UUCP and USENET.* Sebastopol, Calif.: O'Reilly and Associates.

O'Reilly, Tim, and Grace Todino. 1992. *Managing UUCP and USENET.* O'Reilly.

Peek, Jerry. 1989. *MH & xmh: E-Mail for Users and Programmers.* Sebastopol, Calif.: O'Reilly and Associates.

Todino, Grace, and Dale Dougherty. 1991. *Using UUCP and USENET.* O'Reilly.

COMMAND SUMMARY

File permissions
Changing groups (System V)	`newgrp`
Changing permissions	`chmod` *permissions filename*
Changing permission mask	`umask`
Change owner of file	`chown` *new-owner filename(s)*
Change group of file	`chgrp` *new-group filename(s)*

Other users
Who is logged on	`who.`
Writing to other users	`write`
Interactive talking	`talk`
Turning on/off writing	`mesg`
Mail	`mail` or `mailx`

Remote computers
Log-in	`rlogin` *hostname*
	`telnet` *hostname*
File transfer	`rcp` *hostname:source-file destination-file*
	`rcp` *source-file hostname:destination-file*
	`ftp` *hostname*

7 | MULTITASKING

There's a whole lot of things going on

One of the major differences between UNIX and MS-DOS is that under UNIX you can run multiple processes or tasks. Some environments that run on top of MS-DOS, such as Windows and DESQVIEW, permit multiple tasks to be run simultaneously in a MS-DOS environment. MS-DOS itself was designed to run a single program at a time.

PROCESS

A program runs in a UNIX process. Copies of the same program may be executing in multiple processes at the same time. Each process has its own memory address space, a process id, an owner (the user who started the process), a parent process (the process that created it), and a state. A process creates another process which runs another program by the action of spawning. The possible states of a process include running (or ready to run) and waiting (for something to happen). Processes may communicate to each other via pipes that tie together the output of one program to the input of another, with shared files or via other mechanisms.

When you log in, the shell process is created for you. You are the owner of that process. When you execute a command, the shell spawns another process that executes that command. The shell usually waits until that process is complete. Alternatively, the shell can continue executing while the other process is running, so that you have two processes running for you.

Processes for **vi**

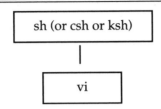

If you use a pipe ('|') to connect two commands, the shell spawns processes for each command. The shell redirects the output of the first command to the input of the second command so that the first is piped to the second. The two processes run independently until the second process performs an input operation. If the first process has not output any characters, the second process waits.

Processes for **cat one.doc | more**

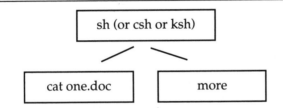

LISTING PROCESSES

The process status command (**ps**) lists the process that you and other users on the system are running. It has many options. The most common are to print full information on each process (**-1**) and to print information on all processes, including ones that are not owned by you (**-a**).[1]

Using **ps** by itself prints a table headed

```
PID TTY STAT TIME COMMAND
```

---

[1] On BSD systems, you do not need the '-' for the options. It is a minor quirk in the convention for options.

The process id is listed under PID. The TTY is the terminal to which the process is connected. The STAT is the state of the process (W = waiting, R = running or runnable, S = sleeping). TIME is the execution time of the process. The command that the process is executing is listed in the COMMAND (or CMD) column.

If you use the -1 option, **ps** lists several additional pieces of information on each process. The UID (user id) is the owner of the process. The parent process (the creator of the process) is listed under PPID. The other columns are valuable to the system administrator and programmers. These include C or CP (the processor utilization—used for scheduling), PRI (priority), NI (nice value—used for priority), ADDR (address of process), SZ (size in blocks of the process), and WCHAN (an event the process is waiting for—if any).

PROCESS PRIORITIES

The computer's central processor can execute only one process at a time.[2] The UNIX operating system schedules which of the processes that are ready to run is executed at any particular time. The schedule is set to timeshare the central processor among processes. This timesharing is very fast, so it usually appears that the processor is executing only your process. If you have a program that performs intensive computations, you may notice a slowdown when there are many other processes running.

Processes are scheduled by the operating system based on priority. Higher-priority processes are scheduled before lower-priority processes. Priorities of processes change, based on how much central processor unit (CPU) time has been used. Processes that use a lot of CPU time get lower priorities. You have some control over the priority of your processes by using the **nice** command. You can execute a command with a lower priority by typing **nice** *amount command*. In UNIX, higher-priority processes have lower-priority numbers and low-priority processes have higher numbers.

It is considered being "nice" to other users to lower the priority of your processes, if you do not need the results immediately. The "nicer" you wish to be, the greater you make the value of *amount*. As a normal user, you cannot be "not-nice" and raise your priority by using a negative value.

BACKGROUND PROCESSES

You can tell the shell to create a process and execute the program without waiting for it to complete by using the background command (**&**). When

---

[2] Computers with multiple CPUs can execute a process on each CPU at the same time.

you type a command, the shell spawns a new process for that command. It then executes the command in the child and waits for the process to terminate. This is similar to MS-DOS, in which COMMAND.COM executes a program and waits for it to finish. You can tell the shell not to wait for the child to finish by typing a **&** at the end of the command. For example,

```
cat *.doc > full.doc &
```

causes a child process to be created and the **cat** command executed in that process. When you type this command, the shell responds by typing the process id of the child. This child process executes in parallel with the shell process. You can use the child process id to select the process on the output of the **ps** command.

The C shell has job control, which allows greater control over how background processes are run. This is described in Chapter 11.

KILLING PROCESSES

You can kill a process for which you are the owner with the **kill** command. This command requires the process id which was reported when it was placed in the background or as reported by the **ps** command.

```
kill process-id
```

Some programs are set up so that the normal **kill** command is ignored. To kill those processes, you need the **-9** or **-KILL** option, as

```
kill -9 process-id
```

or

```
kill -KILL process-id
```

You may get one of two error messages with this command. These are:

No such process	A process with the given id does not exist.
Not owner	You are not the owner of a process, so you cannot kill it.

You can kill all your processes by using a *process-id* of 0. If you kill a process that inputs or outputs to a pipe, the other process will terminate when it attempts to read or write to that pipe.

STARTING A PROCESS AT A LATER TIME

You can delay the execution of a command by using the **at** command. You specify the time at which the command is to run. The syntax varies between BSD and System V. You can enter it as

```
at time
commands
<control-D>
```

The time can be specified with four digits which represent the hours and minutes. You can append an 'a' or 'p' to specify a.m. or p.m. For example, you could run a **cat** command at 9:00 a.m. by typing:

```
at 0900a
cat *.doc > full.doc
<control-D>
```

On some systems, you can use the syntax:

```
at time -c command
```

If *command* contains spaces or punctuation, you need to surround it with quotations marks. You could run the above command as

```
at 0900a -c "cat *.doc > full.doc"
```

Most systems have a way of scheduling a script file (one containing a series of commands).

Workout Multiple processes

1. Print out information on your processes.

```
$ ps
TTY PID              COMMAND
tty process-id       sh
tty process-id       ps
```

The **sh** process is your shell. It may be **csh** or **ksh** if you are running the C shell or the Korn shell. The shell process may not show up on some systems. The **ps** process is the process that is running this command. You may see other processes, especially if you are running on a system with windows.

You may see other columns of information listed, such as "STAT" for state and "TIME" for execution time. The columns may be listed in a different order. The "TTY" heading may read "TT".

2. Start up a process in the background.

```
$ find / -name "xxx" -print > temp &
process-id
```

The **find** program looks for matching filenames in the entire file system. It can take a long time. When the process starts in the background, *process-id* gives the process id.

You may get some error messages as **find** tries to access directories for which you do not have permissions.

3. Print out the processes again.

```
$ ps
TTY      PID
tty  process-id     sh
tty  process-id     find / -name xxx
tty  process-id     ps
```

The **find** process is the background process that you started.

4. Kill the **find** process.

```
$ kill -9 process-id
```

where *process-id* is the number of the **find** process.

6. List the processes again.

```
$ ps
TTY      PID
tty  process-id  sh
tty  process-id  ps
```

7. Start up two processes connected by a pipe in the background.

```
$ find / -name "xxx" -print | more &
process-id
```

8. Print out the processes again.

```
$ ps
TTY      PID
tty      process-id sh
tty      process-id find / -name xxx
tty      process-id more
tty      process-id ps
```

The **find** process is the first background process that you started. The **more** process is the second one. You do not see that the two processes are connected via a pipe.

9. Kill a process.

```
$ kill -9 process-id
```

where *process-id* is the number of the **find** process.

10. List the processes again.

```
$ ps
TTY      PID
tty      process-id sh
tty      process-id ps
```

The **more** process died because the pipe was "broken" when the **find** process was killed.

On some systems, the **more** process may not terminate. You will need to use

```
$ kill -9 process-id
```

where *process-id* is the number of the **more** process.

11. You can spawn another process which uses a shell that differs from your current shell. For example, to use the Bourne shell, enter

```
$ sh
$ ps
tty process-id sh
tty process-id ps
ty process-id sh
```

Note that there is a new process running.

12. Exit from that shell.

```
$ <control-D>
$ ps
tty process-id sh
tty process-id ps
```

The additional process in which the shell was running is gone.

13. Try logging off by killing the shell.

```
$ kill process-id
```

where *process-id* is the process id of the **sh** or **csh** process for which you are the owner.

FOR FURTHER INFORMATION

See the texts listed in Chapter 1.

COMMAND SUMMARY

Processes
    Background processing   **&**
    Listing processes   **ps**
        All processes   **-a**
        Long listing   **-1**
    Changing priority   **nice**
    Killing processes   **kill** *process-id*
    Starting at later time   **at** *time command*
I/O redirection
    Pipe   *command | command*

8 | SHELL PROGRAMMING

It's not just a tool, it's an entire language

The shell program inputs and interprets your keystrokes as commands, much like COMMAND.COM on MS-DOS. You can run any one of a number of shells. The most common are the Bourne, C, and Korn shells. These shells have some features in common, such as the ability to run shell scripts, which work the same as .BAT files in MS-DOS. In this chapter we describe the common aspects of the shells as well as the general tools used in shell scripts.

EXECUTING COMMANDS

The shell interprets and executes the commands that you type in. For commands that are programs, it creates a child process to execute the command. When that process is created, it inherits from its parent shell the environment variables and the current directory. Any change made to environment variables or the current directory in the child process does not change the value in the parent process.

Some commands that you execute on MS-DOS are performed internally by COMMAND.COM. These include DIR, DEL, DATE, and TIME. The other commands are external programs that are run by COMMAND.COM. When the program is done, control returns to COMMAND.COM. UNIX shells work the same way. Only a few commands are performed directly by the shell. All other commands are run in a separate process. The shell normally waits for the other process to complete before continuing. As we have seen in background processing, this does not have to be the case.

One command that the shell executes internally is the change directory command (**cd**). There is a definite reason why it is executed internally. If **cd** were an external command, the shell would create a child process and execute **cd** in that process (which would change the current directory in that process). The shell would wait until that child process was ended. The current directory in the parent process (the one the shell is in) would not be affected!

With MS-DOS, every command returns an exit code, which can be tested in a batch file as ERRORLEVEL. Each UNIX program also returns an exit code, which can be tested in shell scripts. The value of the exit code is zero if the command executed successfully, and some other value if an error occurred. For example, the file comparison program **cmp** compares two files. **cmp** has an exit code of 0 if two files are identical, 1 if the files are different, and 2 if it cannot access one or both files.

THE echo COMMAND

The MS-DOS ECHO command echoes what is on the command line to the screen. The UNIX **echo** does the same thing. It is used in shell scripts to output prompts to the user or to add comments to the output.

```
echo string
```

On many versions of UNIX, **echo** includes a <new-line> end of *string*. If you use the **-n** option, the <new-line> is suppressed; for example,

```
echo -n Enter name
```

yields

```
Enter name
```

with the cursor sitting right after the 'e'.

SCRIPTS

You have used MS-DOS batch (*.BAT) files and may have even written some yourself. Batch files are ASCII text files that list commands to be executed and may include some control statements. The most common statements are the IF and the GOTO. You can pass values to the batch file on the command line. These values can be substituted for parameters in the batch file.

With UNIX, you create script files, which act like MS-DOS batch files. The script files may be just a list of commands or include complex control statements. There is no standard extension for a script file. However, to run the file as a script file, you must have execute permission for it. For example, suppose that you had a file called **dir** that contained

```
echo Directory listing is
ls -l
```

and you had execute permission for it. If you type

```
$ dir
```

the two commands in it would be executed.[1] If you do not have execute permission, you will get an error similar to

```
dir: permission denied
```

or

```
dir: not found
```

SHELL VARIABLES

In MS-DOS, the environment variables are used in a manner similar to both the UNIX environment variables and the shell variables. You can refer to the value of a MS-DOS variable by surrounding it with '%'. For example, if you typed "set MY-VARIABLE=my-value", you could use the value "%MY-VARIABLE%" in a batch file. When you execute a batch file, the values you type on the command line are passed to the batch file. These values can be referred to in the batch file with numeric designations starting with '%', such as "%1", "%2", and "%3".

In UNIX, there are two types of shell variables. The first is the named variable, which is a name with an associated value. You set a named variable with either

```
name=value (sh, ksh)
```

---

[1] The current directory '.' needs to be in the path.

or

> **set** *name*=*value* (csh)

If *value* includes spaces, you surround it with quotation marks. You refer to the value of a named variable by preceding the name with the **$** symbol, as **$***name*. In some cases you may need to use braces around the *name*, such as **${***name***}**. For example, if you set a variable with

> **MY-VALUE="This is my value"** (sh, ksh)

or

> **set MY-VALUE="This is my value"** (csh)

you can refer to it as

> **echo My value is $MY-VALUE**

Shell variables are not passed to a child process. Thus you need to **export** (Bourne, Korn shells) or **setenv** (C shell) the variables so that they may be inherited.

The second type of shell variables are the script arguments, which are the values passed to a shell script. These are two-character symbols starting with **$**. They include **$1**, **$2** to **$9**, which represent the command line arguments.[2] These are the equivalent of the MS-DOS batch file variables %1, %2, and so on.

---

[2] The C shell has a second form for these arguments, such as **argv[1]**, **argv[2]**, and so on.

Workout Script file

1. Use **vi** to create a file called **test-script**.

   $ **vi test-script**

   and enter the following lines in it:

   ```
   echo This is a test script
   echo The parameters are 1:$1 2:$2 3:$3
   ```

```
cat $1 > $2
```

2. Try running the file.

```
$ test-script one.doc out.doc
```

You should get a response similar to

```
test-script: permission denied
```

If you get a message as

```
test-script: not found
```

then make sure . is in **PATH**

```
$ echo $PATH
$ setenv PATH=$PATH\:.    (csh)
$ PATH=$PATH:.    (sh, ksh)
$ export PATH
```

3. Change the file permissions so that it is executable.

```
$ chmod u+x test-script
```

This command adds execute permission for you, the owner of the file.

4. Then run the file as

```
$ test-script one.doc out.doc
```

You should see the following on your screen:

```
This is a test script
The parameters are 1:one.doc 2:out.doc 3:
$
```

5. Do a directory listing of the new file you created by running

```
$ ls o*.doc
one.doc
out.doc
```

As we discussed in earlier chapters, if you surround a string with quotation marks, shell special characters are not interpreted. There is a difference between single and double quotation marks. With double quotes, the special characters are not interpreted, but shell variables are expanded. With single quotes, neither occurs. For example, with the Bourne shell, if you had a script containing

```
set NAME="Sam Hall"
echo The name is $NAME *
echo "The name is $NAME *"
echo 'The name is $NAME *'
```

the output would look like the following:

```
The name is Sam Hall one.doc two.doc three.doc
The name is Sam Hall *
The name is $NAME *
```

In the first **echo**, the * is expanded to matching filenames. In the second echo, there is no filename expansion, but a substitution is made for **$NAME**. With the third **echo**, the string is printed literally.

Workout Shell script

---

1. Create a file called **dir-test**. Its contents will be

   ```
   echo Directory Listing for $1
   ls -l $1
   ```

2. Change the permission on the file to execute

   ```
   $ chmod u+x dir-test
   ```

3. Run the script as

   ```
   $ dir-test *.doc
   one.doc
   ```

   The $1 in the script has been replaced by **one.doc**. The *.doc was expanded by the shell and the script got several parameters.

4. Run the script with

```
$ dir-test "*.doc"
one.doc
out.doc
three.doc
two.doc
```

The ***.doc** was not expanded by the shell when it was passed to **dir-test**. The value of **$1** in the script was ***.doc**. This was then expanded when the shell ran the **ls *.doc** command.

Implicit Concatenation

If you place the value of a variable next to a string or another variable, the two will be concatenated, as

```
FIRST="Sam"
LAST="Hall"
echo $FIRST$LAST
```

outputs **SamHall**. If there might be confusion as to the name of the variable, you should enclose it in braces (**{** and **}**). For example,

```
FIRST="Sam"
echo ${FIRST}Smith
```

If the **echo** statement had been written with **$FIRSTSmith**, the shell would look for a variable with the name **FIRSTSmith**.

PIPES AND FILTERS

Many scripts can be written by combining UNIX programs. The individual commands are referred to as "filters", since they take the input, perform some operation on it, and output the transformed or filtered data. The output of a command may be piped to the input of another command, or redirected to a file. There are some additional options in using the standard input and output with filters.

You can use - as a filename with many commands. This symbol is a synonym for the standard input. For example,

```
cat one.doc - two.doc > merged.doc
```

concatenates **one.doc**, the standard input (the keyboard in this case), and **two.doc** and puts the output into **merged.doc**.

The special file **/dev/tty** acts like the MS-DOS CON file. It is the equivalent of your log-in terminal. So

```
cat one.doc > /dev/tty
```

redirects the output to the terminal screen. This can be useful in shell scripts (described in Chapter 3), to be sure that the output goes to the terminal screen.

The special file **/dev/null** file accepts all input and does nothing with it. For example, if you typed

```
cat one.doc > /dev/null
```

the output from the **cat one.doc** is thrown away. This is useful in shell scripts for programs in which you are not interested in the output, only in the exit value of the program. If input comes from **/dev/null**, the input contains no data. The end-of-file is reached immediately.

COMMAND SYNTAX

You can type two or more commands on a single line by separating them with a semicolon (**;**). If you cannot finish a command on a single line, type **\<Return>** to continue it on the next line.

To run a number of commands in their own subshell, surround the commands with parentheses ( ) . For example,

```
(cd a-directory; cat a-file) \ <Return>
| (cd another-directory; cat > another-file)
```

outputs **a-file** from **a-directory** to the pipe. The second **cat** copies the data from the pipe to **another-file** in **another-directory**.

Script Comments

You can comment shell scripts by using the **#** character. Any text following it is ignored. You should use a comment character followed by a blank line, instead of just a blank line in a script. Some versions of the C shell give errors if there is a blank line. If on the first line of the script you include a one-line comment of the form

```
#!    pathname
```

the shell will spawn the program named by *pathname* and pass to it the name of the script file. This is crucial for running scripts that may be written for different shells or other programs. As discussed in Chapters 10 and 11, the Bourne and C shells have different control syntax. When you write a script that can only run under one of the shells, you should include either

```
#! /bin/sh
```

or

```
#! /bin/csh
```

Conditional Execution of Commands

You may wish to execute two commands in sequence but have the execution of the second command be dependent on the first. If you want one or the other of the two commands, but not both, to execute, you use the OR (| |) punctuator. The syntax is

```
first-command || second-command
```

If *first-command* is successful (i.e., a zero exit code), the *second-command* does not execute. If it is not successful, the *second-command* does execute. The syntax for the AND (**&&**) punctuator is

```
first-command && second-command
```

If *first-command* is successful (i.e., a zero exit code), the *second-command* executes. If it is not successful, the *second-command* does not execute. For example, with

```
cmp one.doc two.doc && echo "Files are the same"
```

the **echo** command executes only if **cmp** is successful (i.e., the files **one.doc** and **two.doc** are exactly the same).

Command Substitution

There is one more form of quotation using backquotes that works well with shell variables. A command that is backquoted makes the output of the command available as a string. For example, the **date** command simply outputs the date and time. So

```
this-date=`date` (sh, ksh)
set this-date = `date` (csh)
```

takes the output of the **date** command and places it into the shell variable **this-date**. You can use command substitution with any command, such as

```
something=`cat one.doc` (sh)
set something=`cat one.doc` (csh)
```

This sets **something** to the output of **cat one.doc**.

Workout Command substitution

1. Make up a file called **list.file** that contains

   ```
   one.doc
   two.doc
   three.doc
   ```

2. Type the following. Note that the quote marks are backquotes.

   ```
   $ ls -l `cat list.file`
   ```

   You will get a listing for those files listed in **list.file**.

SHELL METACHARACTERS

As suggested in Chapter 2, it is usually a good idea not to use punctuation characters in filenames. Since the basics for shells have been covered, the following list simply reviews how the shells use these characters. The characters are referred to in documentation as metacharacters, which are characters with special meanings. To remove the special meaning of a metacharacter, preface it with \ or place it in quotations.

Character Usage

|	Pipe
*	Wildcard for anything
?	Wildcard for single character
[ ]	Sets of characters
[^]	Sets of characters other than those specified
' '	Turns off special character meaning
" "	Turns off meaning but allows parameter substitution
( )	Creates a subshell
$	Prefix to variable name
{ }	Enclosure for variable name
&	Places into background
;	Command separator
\	Turns off meaning of next character
>	Output redirection
> >	Output redirection (appending)
<	Input redirection
| |	Conditional execution
&&	Condition execution
#	Comment
` `	Processes a command and uses output as value

These are metacharacters that have not yet been covered:

@	Computation (csh)
!	History substitution (csh)
%	Make background job foreground (csh, ksh)

The shell also uses:

=	Variable assignment
–	Use as input the output of previous command in pipe

MS-DOS BATCH FILE CONTROLS

The commands in MS-DOS batch files are executed sequentially unless there are control statements. The most common control statement is the IF, which has a variety of test operations. The IF can test if a particular file exists, if a token that is passed to the script is a particular string, or if the exit (error) value of a command is equal to a particular value.

The GOTO statement transfers execution to another line in the batch file. The FOR executes a command iteratively, setting a variable to a different value each time. The PAUSE command outputs a string to the screen and awaits a character. The REM command permits remarks to be part of the executable file. The EXIT command terminates a batch file.

All these batch controls have equivalents in UNIX shell scripts. All three shells have control flow, but their syntax is slightly different. The control syntax for the shells is described in the following chapters.

FOR FURTHER INFORMATION

Kernighan, Brian W., and Rob Pike. 1984. *The UNIX Programming Environment.* Englewood Cliffs, N.J.: Prentice Hall. Programming the Bourne shell, **awk**, and other tools.

Kochan, Stephen G., and Patrick H. Wood. 1989. *UNIX Shell Programming.* Indianapolis, Ind.: Howard W. Sams.

COMMAND SUMMARY

Setting shell variables	*name*=*value* (sh, ksh)
	set *name*=*value* (csh)
Value of shell variables	$*name* or ${*name*}.
Value of script argument	$*number*
Output string	**echo** *string*
Null device	**/dev/null**
Command syntax	
Separator	**;**
Run in subshell	**( )**
Conditional execution	
OR	*first-command* **||** *second-command*
AND	*first-command* **&&** *second-command*
Command substitution	**` `**

9 | TOOLS

There's a tool for every purpose

Many UNIX commands are written to manipulate text. By combining a number of these commands with pipes, very useful operations can be performed without additional programming. Many commands are designed as tools for building pipes. Each performs a single set of related operations. In this chapter we examine a number of tools.

TOOLS IN SCRIPTS

You can test the exit code of these tools in script files. Sometimes you only need the exit code of a command, not the output. Many commands have an option (usually, **-s**) to eliminate output and just return a code. If the command does not have this option, you can redirect the output to **/dev/null** to eliminate its appearance on the screen. As we stated in Chapter 8, the convention for the exit code is that a value of 0 means that the command was successful and any other value means that the command failed in some way. The exit code is also called the status or status code.

With many tools, if you specify a filename as **-**, the standard input will be read. This is useful with programs that are not normally set up to be used as filters in a pipeline.

Tools output errors to the standard error output. These messages include not having access to a file, or files not existing. The default for the error output is the terminal screen. You may wish to redirect the output to another file. The syntax for error redirection varies depending on the shell and is covered in the shell chapters.

There are several flavors of options to UNIX programs. Some options use just single letters following the -, such as -l. Others use multiple characters, such as -d2. The characters following the initial letter are the value associated with that option. In this case, this would set 2 as the value for the -d option. Still others separate the value of the option from the option itself, as -f my-file. In this case, my-file is the value for the -f option.

PATTERN SEARCHING

The **grep** program searches for a pattern of characters in a file or a number of files. It works like the MS-DOS FIND program. It was named for an **ed** command that looked like "g/re/p" which stood for "globally search for a regular expression and print the line". The syntax is

```
grep pattern filename(s)
```

The *pattern* is usually enclosed in quotation marks so that it is not interpreted by the shell as a filename matching pattern. The pattern must be matched on a single line. It cannot span lines in the file.

Regular Expressions

A regular expression appears much like a filename pattern. It uses some of the same syntax, but its meaning as a matching pattern is quite different. Regular expressions are used by **grep**, **vi**, and other programs.

A regular expression consists of a string of characters, some of which may have special meanings. A period (.) matches any character. Braces ([and]) surround a set of characters, which matches any character contained inside. If the left brace is followed by a caret (^), the set of characters is defined to be all those not listed inside. A hyphen can be used to give a range of characters. The \ character turns off the special meaning of the character that follows. For example:

Pattern	Matches
abc	abc
a.c	abc or aac, or a2c, and so on
[abc]	a or b or c
[^abc]	d or e, and so on
\[	[
[a-z]	a or b or c, and so on

The pattern can include a repetition specifier (*). The preceding character or character in a set can occur zero or more times in the matched string. For example:

Pattern	Matches
a*b	**b** or **ab** or **aab** or **aaab** or **aaaaab**, and so on
[ab]*c	**c** or **ac** or **aac** or **bc** or **babac**, and so on
a*	Any string

The last example matches any string since **a** need not be repeated at all. If you want to be sure that the match includes at least one of the characters to be repeated, you will need to repeat it:

Pattern	Matches
aa*b	**ab** or **aab** or **aaab** or **aaaaab**, and so on
[ab][ab]*c	**ac** or **aac** or **bc** or **babac**, and so on

A few more examples of common matches are:

Pattern	Matches
[A-Z][A-Z]*	Strings of uppercase letters
[a-z][a-z]*	Strings of lowercase letters
[0-9][0-9]	Sets of digits
[ ][0-9][0-9][0-9][0-9][0-9][ ]	Five-digit zip codes surrounded by spaces
W.*n	**Washington** or **Wn** or **Wilm-ington** or **Western**

A pattern that includes a repetition specifier will match the longest possible string that matches. However, no matching is done over the <newline> character.

To make a pattern match the start of a line, the ^ is used. To make it match at the end of a line, the $ is used. For example:

Pattern	Matches
^abc	**abc** only if **a** is first character on line
abc$	**abc** only if **c** is last character on line

Your system may have international capabilities. In this event, you can use names rather than ranges for particular sets of characters. You specify these sets with:

[:*type*:]

where *type* may be **lower, upper, digit, cntrl** (control), **space, alpha** (alphabetic) or **alnum** (alphanumeric). Other types may be available on your system.

This symbol is used inside of brackets (**[ ]**). For example, you could look for strings of lowercase characters with:

```
grep "[[:lower:]][[:lower:]]*" one.doc
```

Workout grep

1. Search **presidents** for any names with **ad** in either case.

```
$ grep "[Aa][Dd]" presidents
```

2. Search **presidents** for names containing **W**.

```
$ grep "W" presidents
```

3. Search **presidents** for last names beginning with **W**. These are the strings that follow the numeric order.

```
$ grep "[0-9][0-9]*  *W" presidents
```

[0-9][0-9]* *W matches any number of digits followed by any number of spaces followed by **W**.

4. Search the **/etc/passwd** file for your user name.

```
$ grep your-user-name /etc/passwd
```

You may not get any matches, depending on whether your system is part of a network. Your user information may be kept in a file other than **/etc/passwd**. In that case, try looking for the user named **root** with:

```
$ grep root /etc/passwd
```

You can specify a number of options with **grep**. To print only a count of the matching lines, use **-c**. For only the names of the files in which there was a matching line, use **-l**. To ignore case on matches, use **-i**. To reverse the test and print out lines not containing the pattern, use **-v** (for invert). **grep** returns a status code of zero if there was at least one matching line. For example

grep -c W presidents	outputs count of lines containing **W**
grep -l test *	outputs filenames of files containing **test**
grep -i ad presidents	outputs lines containing **ad** in either case
grep -v a presidents	outputs lines not containing **a**

There are two variations of **grep**, called **fgrep** and **egrep**. The **fgrep** command can quickly search for multiple strings simultaneously. The **egrep** command has additional pattern characters. These include symbols for one or more occurrences of a character (**+**) and zero or more occurrences (**?**). **egrep** has the ability to group regular expressions with ( ) and to give alternative regular expressions with |. It is also the fastest of the three programs.

THE STREAM EDITOR

The stream editor (**sed**) processes a number of editing commands on a file. It is useful in a pipeline. Some commands include substitution and line modification. The syntax is

> **sed -f** *command-file filename*

or

> **sed** *immediate-commands filename*

If you specify the **-f** *command-file* option, the commands are read from *command-file*. If you do not, the **sed** commands are taken from the command line. If you do not specify *filename,* then **sed** operates on the standard input. The basic syntax is

> *pattern-or-lines command*

The *command* is executed for every line that matches *pattern-or-lines*. If you do not specify a *pattern-or-lines*, the command is performed for every line in the input file.

The substitution command to change an expression is

`s/`*old-expression*`/`*new-expression*`/`

For example,

`s/Bush/Clinton/`

changes the first occurrence of "Bush" on every line to "Clinton". To change every occurrence on every line, the syntax is

`s/`*old-expression*`/`*new-expression*`/g`

For example,

`s/Bush/Clinton/g`

changes every occurrence of "`Bush`" on every line to "`Clinton`".

Patterns or Lines in `sed`

When executing a command, you can specify a line number, a range of line numbers, or a pattern. You designate either a line number or a range using the syntax

```
number
first-number,last-number
```

For example,

`1,10s/Bush/Clinton/g`

applies the substitution only to lines 1 through 10. The `$` symbol is used to represent the last line in the file. For example,

`20,$s/Bush/Clinton/g`

applies the substitution from line 20 to the end of the file.
You can specify lines using a regular expression as

`/`*expression*`/`

For example,

```
/President/s/Bush/Clinton/g
```

will substitute "Clinton" for "Bush" only on lines that contain a match to the pattern "President".

If this command were in a file called succeed.sed and you wanted to change one.doc, you would run the sed with

```
sed -f succeed.sed one.doc
```

The output would be one.doc with the substitutions made. You could also run this on the command line with

```
sed '/President/s/Bush/Clinton/g' one.doc
```

```
A useful sed command is
```

```
sed 's/  */ /'
```

This replaces any number of spaces on the standard input by a single space on the standard output.

Replacement Strings in sed

You can perform complex replacements using the string that matches a pattern. You specify the matching string with &. For example, the command

```
s/19[0-9]*/"&"/
```

will replace every occurrence of a string of digits beginning with "19" with the same string surrounded by quotation marks.

If you bracket portions of the regular expression with \ (and \ ), the corresponding matching string can be used in the replacement using \number. For example, the command

```
s/chapter \([0-9][0-9]*\)/section \1/
```

replaces "chapter" with "section" wherever it is followed by at least one digit. The digit string that matches \([0-9][0-9]*\) is substituted for \1 in the replacement string. If you had more than a single bracketed expression, the replacement values would be \1, \2, and so on.

Other sed Commands

You delete lines with the d command. For example:

```
/Bush/d
```

deletes every line in which "**Bush**" appears. You append lines to a file using command **a** or **i**. Until one is found not ending in \, all the following lines are inserted into the file. To read a file for lines to insert, use **r** *filename.*

You quit processing the input with the **q** command. For example,

```
sed '3q' one.doc
```

will print the first three lines of a file and then quit.

The default action for **sed** is to print every line, regardless of what happened to it (unless it was deleted). You can use the **-n** option to change the action so as not to print the lines. The print command **p** is then used to print the lines. For example,

```
sed -n '/Bush/p' one.doc
```

prints only the lines containing "**Bush**".

Workout sed

1. Output **one.doc** with all instances of "the" as "The".

```
$ sed 's/the/The/g' one.doc
```

SORTING COMMAND

The **sort** command sorts the standard input to the standard output. It works somewhat like the MS-DOS SORT command. If you type

```
sort < one.doc > one.sorted
```

each line in **one.doc** is sorted by ascending ASCII value to **one.sorted**. You can also specify the name of the file to be sorted on the command line.

Uppercase letters have values that are less than lowercase. For example, suppose that the input file contained these four lines:

```
paul
George
Sam
al
```

The output file would be sorted as

```
George
Sam
al
paul
```

To specify that upper- and lower-case should be folded together, use the -f option. Then the output file would be look like

```
al
George
paul
Sam
```

You can sort in reverse order with the **-r** option. With this option, the output file would look like

```
paul
al
Sam
George
```

sort will eliminate duplicate lines in the output with the **-u** option.

Sort can work on fields as well as lines. Each line is broken into fields by field separators. The default field separator is the space. You set another character to be the field separator with **-t**character. To identify which field to sort on, you specify the field offset. The first field has an offset of 0. The **+**field-offset option specifies the field. For example, to sort by the second field, you would use **+1** as the option. The field will be sorted by character order unless the numeric option **n** is specified. For example,

sort +3

sorts the input file by the fourth field. The command

sort +3n

sorts the input file by the fourth field in numeric order.

Workout sort

1. Sort the **presidents** file with

```
$ sort presidents | more
```

Note that it is ordered by ASCII order. The first lines contain numbers 1, 10, 11, and so on.

2. Sort the **presidents** file with

```
$ sort +0 presidents | more
```

The output appears just as in the previous step. It is sorted on the first field, but the field is treated as a string of characters.

3. Sort the **presidents** file with

```
$ sort +0n presidents | more
```

The output is now numerically sorted. The first lines contain numbers 1, 2, 3, 4, and so on.

4. Sort the file by last name with

```
$ sort +1 presidents | more
```

UNIQUE LINES

The **uniq** program outputs only lines that are not duplicated in a file. To be eliminated, the duplicated lines must be adjacent in the file. **uniq** has several useful options. It outputs only the duplicated lines with the **-d** option. It outputs only the lines that are unique (i.e., not duplicated) with the **-u** option. It counts the occurrences of each line with the **-c** option. For example, if the **test** file contained

```
one
two
two
three
```

then **uniq test** would output

```
one
two
three
```

The command **uniq** **-u** would output

```
one
three
```

The command **uniq** **-c** would output

```
1: one
2: two
1: three
```

COMPARING TWO FILES

The **comm** program compares two sorted files and determines what lines are in common and which are unique to each file. **comm** outputs three columns. The first is for lines occurring only in first file, the second for those only in second file, and the third for common lines. For example,

```
comm one.doc two.doc
```

compares **one.doc** to **two.doc**.

You can suppress the output of lines using options. To eliminate the lines showing the first file, use **-1**; to eliminate the second file lines, use **-2**; to eliminate the common lines, use **-3**. For example,

```
comm -12 one.doc two.doc
```

prints only the lines that are in both **one.doc** and **two.doc**.[1] Note that the files must be sorted in order for **comm** to work properly. If they are not, the comparison will be erroneous.

---

[1] The **diff** program also compares two files. It is described in Chapter 14.

Workout **comm**

---

1. Sort **one.doc** and **two.doc**.

```
$ sort one.doc > one.doc.sorted
$ sort two.doc > two.doc.sorted
```

2. Find out what lines are common.

```
$ comm one.doc.sorted two.doc.sorted
```

3. List only the common lines.

```
$ comm -12 one.doc.sorted two.doc.sorted
```

4. Try comparing the unsorted files

```
$ comm -12 one.doc two.doc
```

Note that you do not get any common lines, as the files are unsorted.

TRANSLATING CHARACTERS

The translation program (`tr`) substitutes characters for other characters. You specify a list of characters to be changed along with a corresponding list into which to change them. `tr` reads only the standard input. Its syntax is

```
tr set-of-characters set-of-characters
```

For example, the command

```
tr "abc" "xyz" < one.doc
```

outputs the contents of **one.doc** with each "**a**" changed to "**x**", each "**b**" changed to "**y**", and each "**c**" changed to "**z**". If the second `set-of-characters` is shorter than the first, the last character in the second set is used as the substitution for the remaining characters in the first set. The command

```
tr "abc" "x" < one.doc
```

substitutes "**x**" for every occurrence of "**a**", "**b**", and "**c**". You can specify ranges of characters using a hyphen. For example,

```
tr "A-Z" "a-z" < one.doc
```

changes all uppercase characters to lowercase.

If you need to pass a control character as a token to **tr**, you use the escape character (\), followed by the octal representation. For example, "\012" is the string containing the <new-line> character. For example,

```
tr "\012" " " < one.doc
```

translates every <new-line> to <space>.

There are several options to **tr**. To complement the first set of characters, use the **-c** option. **tr** squeezes all sets of repeated characters to single characters with the **-s** option. It deletes all the matching input characters, rather than replacing them with the **-d** option. For example,

```
tr -sc "A-Za-z" "\012" < one.doc
```

changes all characters that are not alphabetical to <new-line>s (value '\012') and outputs only one <new-line> for each set of <new-line>s. This outputs every word in **one.doc** on a separate line.

```
tr -d "\012" < one.doc
```

outputs **one.doc** with every <new-line> deleted.

Your system may be internationalized. In this case, you can refer to sets of characters using the same names as **grep**. You could change all uppercase characters to lowercase with

```
tr "[:upper:]" "[:lower:]" < one.doc
```

COLLECTING FILES

We have already used the **cat** command for typing files. It is useful for collecting files that are to be part of a pipeline. For example,

```
cat one.doc two.doc | tr "A-Z" "a-z"
```

concatenates **one.doc** and **two.doc** to standard output, which is then piped to the **tr** command.

HEADS AND TAILS OF FILES

The **head** and **tail** programs output the first lines and last lines of a file, respectively. By default, these output the first 10 or the last 10 (or four) lines. You can output *number* lines by specifying *-number* option. For example,

```
head -2 one.doc
```

prints out the first two lines of **one.doc** and

```
tail -20 presidents
```

prints out the last 20 lines of **presidents**.

CUTTING SELECTED FIELDS OR COLUMNS

The **cut** program cuts a set of columns or fields out of a file. It may not be available on your UNIX system. You specify columns to be cut with the -c*column-list* option. The *column-list* is a set of column numbers separated by commas. It can include ranges using a hyphen. For example,

```
cut -c1-3,5-10
```

cuts columns 1 through 3 and columns 5 through 10 of every line of the standard input and puts them on the output.
   You can cut fields with the -f*field-list* option. The default field delimiter is the <tab>, but you can set it with the -d*delimiter-character* option, for example **-d:** sets a colon delimiter. If you use a space character as a delimiter in a file, you need to put the option in the quotes, as **"-d "**. Otherwise, the shell will just pass "-d" to the **cut** program and you will get an error from it. Depending on the system, the default delimiter may be <tab> or <space>. For example,

```
cut -f2  "-d " presidents
```

cuts the second field (the last name) out of each line in the **presidents** file and outputs to the standard output.

PASTING FILES

The **paste** command pastes two files together. This command is not found on all UNIX systems. **paste** treats corresponding lines in each file as columns. You can specify the same file as input multiple times. The syntax is

```
paste file-1 file-2 ...
```

The columns are delimited with <tab>, but you can set the delimiter to a different character with the **-d**_delimiter_ option. For example,

```
paste one.doc two.doc
```

will output lines, each containing the contents of the corresponding lines in one.doc and two.doc.

```
paste -d: one.doc two.doc
```

will cause each line to contain a ":" between the line from one.doc and the line from two.doc.

Workout cut and paste

1. Cut the first and second fields out of presidents.

```
$ cut -f1 "-d " presidents > order.txt
$ cut -f2 "-d " presidents > last-name.txt
```

2. Paste the two files back together.

```
$ paste -d: last-name.txt order.txt > name-order.txt
```

3. See what the result looks like.

```
$ more name-order.txt
```

WALKING THE DIRECTORY TREE

The MS-DOS XCOPY command can walk the directory tree and copy all files in subdirectories with the "/S" option. Some vendors supply MS-DOS programs, such as FILEFIND, that can search an entire disk for files with particular names. UNIX has a command that performs similar functions but which is more general purpose. The command **find** allows printing of filenames, or executing programs on filenames that match particular criteria. Its syntax is

```
find directory expression
```

The program starts at *directory* and looks at each filename found in that directory and all subdirectories. For each file it then checks the parameters given in *expression*. The *expression* is made up of selection criteria and execution operations. For example, **-name** *"*.doc"* selects those files whose names match the ***.doc** pattern. The **-print** operation prints the name of the current file. To print the names of all files in the current directory and subdirectories, use

```
find . -print
```

To select those with filenames matching *"*.doc"* and print them out, use

```
find . -name "*.doc" -print
```

If you do not use **-print**, nothing will be printed. Some versions of **find** output the matching filenames without the need for **-print**. Note that if you did not include quotations around ***.doc**, the shell will perform filename matching. For example,

```
find . -name *.doc -print
```

may yield a "find: Illegal expression" error. What **find** actually sees looks similar to

```
find . -name one.doc two.doc three.doc -print
```

If you typed the command as

```
find . -print -name "*.doc"
```

all filenames will be printed out. The criteria and operations in the expression are evaluated in the order in which they are listed on the command line. Since **-print** comes first, it is performed before the matching for **-name** *"*.doc"*. If you entered

```
find . -print -name "*.doc" -print
```

the output would contain all the filenames with those matching *"*.doc"* being duplicated.

Selection criteria include the owner (**-user**) and the modification time (**-mtime**). For example, to select files that are owned by you, anywhere in the file system, you could use

```
find / -user user-id -print
```

Another criterion is the execution operation. You give a command to be executed for each filename that is matched with **-exec**. To specify the current matched filename, you use the symbol **{ }** in the command. The command must end with a semicolon, which is preceded by the escape character to avoid it being interpreted by the shell. For example,

```
find . -name "*.bak" -exec rm {} \;
```

executes the **rm** command for each file matching "***.bak**".

Instead of using the **-exec** feature of **find**, you could use the command substitution feature of the shell. For example,

```
find . -name "*.bak" -print > backup-files
rm `cat backup-files`
```

performs the same operations as those performed in the previous example.

Workout find

1. See if anyone else on your system has files matching ***.doc**. First switch to your home directory

```
$ cd
```

2. Then type

```
$ find .. -name "*.doc" -print
```

You may get a number of error messages as **find** tries to access directories for which you do not have the necessary permissions.

COMPARING FILES

The **cmp** program compares two files on a character-by-character basis using **cmp**. This works like the MS-DOS COMP command. It prints the first difference and then exits. For example,

```
cmp one.doc two.doc
```

compares `one.doc` to `two.doc`. This is a quick way to be sure that two files match, regardless of type.

WORD COUNT

The `wc` program counts the number of words, lines, and characters in a file. It outputs these three counts. A word is a string of characters surrounded by white space. A line ends with a new-line character or the end-of-file. `wc` counts only characters with the `-c` option; only words with `-w`; and only lines with `-1`. For example,

```
wc -1 one.doc
```

prints the number of lines in `one.doc`.

TEE

The `tee` command can save intermediate output within a pipeline. It copies the input to the output and also writes a copy of the input to a file. For example,

```
cat one.doc | tee one.save | grep "a"
```

The `one.doc` file is output to `tee`, which passes the data to `grep`. `tee` also creates a copy in `one.save`.

The `tee` command is useful for debugging pipelines to see what is occurring.

DATE AND TIME

The `date` command outputs the current date and time. You type

```
date
```

WAITING

The `sleep` command waits a given amount of time. It is useful in shell scripts to delay execution of a command. A script containing this command is normally run in the background. Otherwise, the shell will wait for the script to complete. The syntax is

```
sleep seconds-to-wait
```

For example, the script

```
echo I am going away for 60 seconds
sleep 60
echo Time to get up
```

will output **Time to get up** 60 seconds after you start it. You can remind yourself to do something in 15 minutes with

```
(sleep 900; echo Get coffee) &
```

As shown in previous chapters, the (and) symbols put this command into a subshell and the & runs this subshell in the background.

Workout Tools

---

1. Try each of the commands listed in this chapter and see if you get what you expect.
2. Create a script named **who-there** to count how many users are on the system. It might look like

```
echo -n "Number of users currently on system "
who | wc -l
```

Be sure to make it executable with

```
$ chmod u+x who-there
```

The quotes are needed around the words to **echo** so that a space will be echoed at the end of the line. Your version of **wc** may output spaces prior to the count, so the space at the end of the line might not be necessary.

The **who** command lists all users currently logged in. The **wc -l** counts the number of lines in the output that **who** produces.
3. Run the script with

```
    $ who-there
```

4. Alter the script to include **tee** as

```
echo -n Number of user currently on system
who | tee temp | wc -l
```

5. Run the script with

```
    $ who-there
```
Then look at the **temp** file that was created.

6. Try running this script and look at its intermediate files.

```
$ cat one.doc | tr -cs "A-Za-z0-9" "\012"\<return>
| tee temp1 | tr "A-Z" "a-z" | tee temp2 <return>
| sort -u > temp3
```

The final output in **temp3** is a list of unique words in the **one.doc** file.

FOR FURTHER INFORMATION

Dougherty, Dale. 1989. **sed** *and* **awk**. Sebastopol, Calif.: O'Reilly and Associates.

Holsberg, Peter. 1992. *UNIX Desktop Guide to Tools*. Sams.

Peek, Jerry, Tim O'Reilly, and Mike Loukides. 1993. *UNIX Power Tools*. O'Reilly/Bantam.

or the guides listed in Chapter 1.

COMMAND SUMMARY

Pattern searching	**grep** *pattern filename(s)*
Count of matching lines	`-c`
Names of the files	`-l`
Ignore case on matches	`-i`
Print lines not in pattern	`-v`
Pattern searching: simultaneous	**fgrep**
Pattern searching: extended	**egrep**

Stream editor	**sed -f** *command-file filename*
	sed *immediate-commands filename*
Substitution	**s/**old-expression/new-expression/
Global substitution	**s/**old-expression/new-expression/**g**
Line specification	*number*
	first-number,last-number
	/expression/
	/first-expression/,/second-expression/
Replacement string	**&**
Replacement strings	\(\) \number
Deleting lines	**d**
Appending	**a** or **i**
Reading a file	**r** *filename*
Quit processing	**q**
Sorting files	**sort**
Field sort	**+**field-offset
Field delimiter	**-t**character.
Numeric sort	**-n**
Unique lines	**uniq**
Compare two files	**comm** *first-file second-file*
Translate characters	**tr** *set-of-characters set-of-characters*
Collecting files	**cat** *filename(s)*
Head of file	**head**
Tail of file	**tail**
Cut selected fields	
or columns	**cut**
Columns	**-c**column-list
Fields	**-f**field-list
Field delimiter	**-d**delimiter-character
Pasting files	**paste** *file-1 file-2* ...
Walk directory tree	**find** *directory expression*
Name criteria	**-name** *pattern*
Print criteria	**-print**
Owner criteria	**-user**
Modification time	**-mtime**
Execute criteria	**-exec**
Replacement within	
execute	**{}**
Comparing files	**cmp** *first-file second-file*
Word count	**wc**
Characters count	**-c**
Word count	**-w**
Line count	**-l**

Tee	**tee** *filename*
Date and time	**date**
Waiting	**sleep** *seconds-to-wait*
Command substitution	` ` ` `
Regular expressions	
Any character	.
Set of characters	[ ]
Set of characters not specified	[^]
Escape character	\
Zero or more previous character	*
Beginning of line	^
End of line	$
(egrep only)	
one or more occurrences	+
zero or more occurrences	?
expression grouping	( )
alternative expressions	|

10 | BOURNE SHELL

The original language

The Bourne shell (**sh**) is available on all UNIX systems. Many system administration scripts are written in this shell. Shell variables and shell flow control are described here. The Korn shell has the same basic syntax as the Bourne shell, with some extensions.

BOURNE SHELL USAGE

The default prompt for the Bourne shell is **#**. If the **sh** is specified in the **/etc/passwd** file as your log-in shell, you will get this prompt. You can change this by setting the **$PS1** variable.

The prompt that you normally see is the value of **PS1**. A different prompt (the value of **PS2**) will appear if the shell determines that a command line is not complete. For example, if you typed the following, the prompt changes.

```
$ cat '<Return>
>
```

The '**>**' is the secondary prompt. The shell is telling you that you have not completed a command and is asking you for more input. In this case, it is due to the unmatched quotes.

The **.profile** file is executed by the Bourne shell the first time you log-in. It usually contains commands that set the values for variables such as **PS1** and **PS2**.

To execute a shell script in the same process as that used by the current shell, use the **.** statement, as

> **.** *script-file*

Executing in the same process is needed if *script-file* contains settings for shell or environment variables. For example, to test out a new **.profile** file without logging off, you would type

> **.** **.profile**

If you typed

> **.profile**

a new child process would be created. Any changes in the shell or environment variable would be made in that process. When it exits, the changes would not be reflected back into the parent process.

When writing Bourne shell scripts, you should include a comment on the first line in the form

> **#! /bin/sh**

If the script is run by another type of shell, that shell will spawn a **sh** program to execute the script. This is necessary since the syntax for control flow is different between shells.

Redirecting Standard Error

With the Bourne and Korn shells, standard error output is redirected with **2>** *filename*. So

> **cat xxxx 2> error-file**

outputs any error messages to **error-file**. You can redirect it to go to the same place as standard output with **2>&1**. Alternatively, you can redirect standard output to go to the same place as the standard error output with **1>&2**. This feature is useful inside scripts to be sure that error messages are displayed on the terminal even if the output for the script itself was redirected. For example, if a script contained

```
echo "An error occurred in the script" 1>&2
```

the output will be displayed on the terminal screen even if the standard output for the script was redirected.

SHELL VARIABLES

As shown in Chapter 9, to set a named variable, type the name followed by equals sign followed by the value. These three items must appear together without any spaces or tabs.

```
name=value
```

as in

```
my-name=Sam
```

If the value you wish to give the variable contains spaces, use quotes around the value, as

```
my-name="Sam Hall"
```

To refer to a named variable, use $ followed by the name, such as

```
echo $my-name
```

To remove a named variable, type just the name and an equals sign.

```
name=
```

To print out the values of all the shell variables, type **set**.
    To export a shell variable to the environment, you use

```
export name
```

such as

```
export my-name
```

If you do not export the variable, it will not be part of the environment in any child processes.

When the shell first executes, it reads the environment variables and creates shell variables with the same name and values. For example, suppose that you typed

```
MY-VARIABLE="xxx"
export MY-VARIABLE
sh
```

In the child process running **sh**, there will be a shell variable named **MY-VARIABLE** with the value **xxx**. The shell uses the value of the shell variable **PATH** for the path to search for commands to execute.

There are several other symbolic variables that are set by the shell. These include the exit status of last command (**$?**), the process number of the last command placed in background (**$!**), and the process number of the current shell (**$$**). The value of **$$** is useful for generating unique temporary filenames.

Shell Variables within a Script

The shell variables that are passed to a script are designated as **$1**, **$2**, and so on. The value of **$0** is the name by which the script was executed. There are three additional shell variables whose values are set. The number of parameters passed to a shell script is **$#**. The list of parameters as a single string is **$@**. A list of parameters as separate strings is **$***. The **$*** variable acts the same as **$@** unless it is quoted. We shall see the difference between these two shortly.

Only the values of **$1** through **$9** are accessible inside the script. If you call a script with 10 arguments, the first nine will be assigned to these variables. Like the MS-DOS SHIFT command, you can execute **shift** to shift the variable values by one position. The value of **$1** takes on the value of **$2**, **$2** takes on **$3**, and so on. The value of **$9** takes on the value of the next argument that was passed. The value of **$#** is decremented by one each time you shift.

Reading Variables from Standard Input

Inside a script you may need to input values from the user. The **read** command reads a line from standard input and places the values it finds into the variables whose names are listed. The syntax is

```
read    variable-1 variable-2 ...
```

If you specify only *variable-1*, the value of the entire line is placed in that variable. If you specify *variable-1* and *variable-2*, the part of the string up to the first white space (spaces or tabs) is placed in *variable-1*. The remainder of the string after the white space is placed in *variable-2*. If you specify enough variables, each part of the string that is separated by white space will be placed in a separate variable. For example, if you had in your script

```
echo Enter a filename
read filename
```

the user would see

```
Enter a filename
```

and the cursor would be waiting on the next line. If the user typed

```
one.doc
```

the value of `$filename` would become **one.doc**. If the user typed

```
one.doc two.doc
```

the value of `$filename` would become **one.doc two.doc**. If the script had

```
echo Enter a filename
read filename1 filename2
```

and the user typed

```
one.doc two.doc
```

the value of `$filename1` would be **one.doc** and the value of `$filename2` would be **two.doc**.

Workout Script

Note: This workout assumes that you only have four files that match ***.doc** in the current directory. You may have more than four. If you type **ls *.doc**, you will get a list of the files. The name of the first file in the list should replace **one.doc** wherever it appears in this workout.

1. Run the previous `dir-test` script (from Chapter 8) with

   ```
   $ dir-test one.doc out.doc two.doc three.doc
   ```

   Only a listing for `one.doc` appears, as the remaining parameters are not used.
2. Run the script as

   ```
   $ dir-test *.doc
   ```

   Only the listing for `one.doc` is printed. The shell expands `*.doc` so that the call to `dir-test` looks just as in the preceding step.
3. Run the script as

   ```
   $ dir-test "*.doc"
   ```

   A listing for `one.doc`, `out.doc three.doc`, and `two.doc` is created.
4. Create a file called `dir-test1`. This should contain

   ```
   #! /bin/sh
   echo Directory Listing for $@
   echo Number of arguments is $#
   ls -l $@
   ```

   Remember to `chmod u+x dir-test1`.
5. Run the script with

   ```
   $ dir-test1 *.doc
   ```

   You get a listing for all matching files and an argument count equal to the number of matching files.
6. Run the script again with

   ```
   $ dir-test1 "*.doc"
   ```

   You will get a listing for all matching files and an argument count of 1.

CONTROL STATEMENTS

As mentioned earlier, MS-DOS has several control statements for use in scripts. We cover the Bourne shell control statements here.

`if` Statement

The `if` statement performs a set of commands if the result of a command is true. The value of zero is considered to be true. A nonzero value is considered to be true. Every program returns an exit code that can be tested with the `if`. The syntax is

```
if   test-command
    then
        commands
fi
```

The **cmp** command return the value of zero if the two files are the same. So you could have a script such as

```
if cmp -s one.doc two.doc
    then
    echo The two files are same
fi
```

The **-s** option was supplied to **cmp**, so it only returned an exit code.

Test Program

The **test** program provides a number of tests on strings, files, and other values. **test** returns an exit value that can be tested with the `if` and other statements. When you execute **test**, you pass it parameters that represent the test you wish to perform. For example

```
test $1 = "astring"
```

checks the value of `$1` for equality to the value "**astring**". If they are equal, **test** returns a zero (for true). You could use this in an `if` as

```
if test $1 = "astring"
    then
    echo First token is astring
fi
```

There is a shorthand form for using the test command, the [command.[1] If you use this shorthand, you need to terminate the test command with a]. The [and] must be separated from all other characters by spaces. The statements above would look as follows:

```
if [ $1 = "astring" ]
    then
    echo First token is astring
fi
```

There are numerous items that can be tested. These are listed in Table 10–1. For example,

```
if test -f $1
then
    echo File $1 exists
fi
```

tests to see if the first argument is the name of an existing file.

Be sure to include spaces around all these operators. Otherwise the operator will be considered as part of the preceding name or value. You will get error messages from **test** if you fail to include the spaces.

Since $? is the exit status for the previous command, you could program the example in the preceding section as

```
cmp -s one.doc two.doc
if [ $? = 0 ]
    then
    echo The two files are same
fi
```

There is a difference between string tests and arithmetic tests. A test such as:

```
test 0 = 000
```

is false, since the strings are not the same. However,

```
test 0 -eq 000
```

is true, since both sides of the **-eq** evaluate to the same numeric value.

---

[1] The file named [is actually linked to **test**.

TABLE 10–1 Tests

Test if string is not null	*string*
Test if file exists	**-f** *filename*
Test if file is a directory	**-d** *filename*
Test if file is readable	**-r** *filename*
Test if file is writable	**-w** *filename*
Test if file is executable	**-x** *filename* [2]
Test if file size greater than zero	**-s** *filename*
Test if file is named pipe	**-p** *filename* [2]
Test if string has length zero	**-z** *string*
Test if string has non-zero length	**-n** *string*
Test if strings are identical	*string-1* **=** *string-2*
Test if strings are not identical	*string-1* **!=** *string-2*
Test of numeric values	*number-1 operator number-2*
operator is	
Equal	**-eq**
Not equal	**-ne**
Greater than	**-gt**
Greater than or equal	**-ge**
Less than	**-lt**
Less than or equal	**-le**
Logical operators	
Negation (not)	**!**
AND	**-a**
OR	**-o**
Grouping	**(** *expression* **)**

[2] Some versions do not have these tests.

Workout Making a backup copy with editing

1. Enter the following script as **editor**.

```
#! /bin/sh
if [ -f $1 ]
    then
```

```
        cp $1 $1.bak
   fi
   vi $1
```

2. Try running this on **presidents**:

   $ **editor presidents**

   After you are finished editing, list the directory and note what is new with

   $ **ls**

---

else Statement

The **else** clause can be used inside an **if** for commands you want executed when the test condition is false. The syntax is

```
if   test-command
     then
          commands
     else
          commands
fi
```

for example,

```
if cmp -s one.doc two.doc
     then
          echo The two files $1 and $2 are same
     else
          echo The two files $1 and $2 are different
fi
```

elif Statement

The **elif** statement permits a multiple set of **if** tests. It combines an **else** with an **if**. It is used inside an **if,** for example,

```
if cmp -s one.doc two.doc
```

```
    then
    echo one.doc and two.doc match
elif cmp -s one.doc three.doc
    then
    echo one.doc and three.doc match
elif cmp -s two.doc three.doc
    then
    echo two.doc and three.doc match
fi
```

The first time **cmp** returns true, the appropriate response is output.

Exit Script

The **exit** statement terminates the script and returns the value that follows it as the exit code. The syntax is

```
exit value
```

A proper script should be terminated with an **exit** and a value. If it terminates by reaching the end of the file, the value it returns may vary every time it executes.

Workout if

---

1. This shell script interprets MS-DOS commands and executes the appropriate UNIX command. Enter in a file called **ms-dos**.

```
#! /bin/sh
if [ $# -ne 2 ]
    then
    echo Usage: ms-dos command filename
    exit 1
fi
if [ $1 = "dir" ]
    then
    echo Directory of $2
    ls -l $2
elif [ $1 = "type" ]
    then
    echo File listing of $2
```

```
        cat $2
    else
        echo Unknown command $1
    fi
    exit 0
```

2. Run this command as

```
$ ms-dos dir one.doc
$ ms-dos dir *.doc
$ ms-dos dir "*.doc"
$ ms-dos type one.doc
```

Note the differences between what is output in these four operations. Compare this to the first Workout in this chapter.

for Statement

The **for** statement works like the FOR statement in MS-DOS. One or more commands are repeated with a different value substituted for an index each repetition. The syntax looks like

```
for index in list
    do
    commands
    done
```

An example is

```
for name in one.doc two.doc three.doc
    do
    echo File is $name
    cat $name
    done
```

The **for** loop will be executed three times. The first time, the value of **$name** will be **one.doc**; the second time, **two.doc**; and the third time, **three.doc**.

You can use the **for** statement to access each parameter that is passed to the script by not including a list. This syntax is

```
for index
    do
    commands
    done
```

The **for** loop repeats once for each argument to the script. For example, suppose that you had a script named **for-script** containing

```
for name
    do
    echo File is $name
    cat $name
    done
```

If you executed **for-script** with

```
for-script one.doc two.doc three.doc
```

it would have the same output as that of the previous example.

Workout `for`

1. Write a script that determines if a set of files exists. Call it **exists**. It could look like

```
for name
    do
    if [ -f $name ]
      then
      echo $name exists
    else
      echo $name does not exist
    fi
    done
```

2. Try it out with

```
$ exists one.doc two.doc xxxx
```

Looping with the `while` Statement

You can execute a number of commands repeatedly with the **while** statement. The syntax is

```
while test-command
    do
        commands
    done
```

If `test-command` returns true, the `commands` are executed. The `test-command` is run again, and if it still returns true, the loop is reexecuted: for example,

```
name=anything
while [ "$name" ]
    do
    echo Enter filename to type
    read name
    if [ "$name" ]
        then
        cat "$name"
    fi
    done
```

This script will loop, each time asking for a filename to pass to **cat**. If the user just enters <Return>, **$name** will have no characters in it. The loop will exit since [**"$name"**] will be false.

If you want your loop to execute while a condition is false, use **until** in place of **while**.

Workout `while`

1. This shell script interprets MS-DOS commands and executes the appropriate UNIX command. Enter in a file called **ms-dos-loop**.

```
#! /bin/sh
not-done=1
while [ $not-done = 1 ]
    do
    echo Enter command
```

```
        read command
        echo Enter filename
        read filename
        if [ $command = "dir" ]
            then
            echo Directory of $filename
            ls -l $filename
        elif [ $command = "type" ]
            then
            echo Listing of $filename
            cat $filename
        elif [ $command = "exit" ]
            then
            not-done=0
        else
            echo Unknown command $command
        fi
        done
    exit 0
```

2. Run this script as:

```
ms-dos-loop
```

Try entering the command **dir** three times with the following as arguments:

```
one.doc
*.doc
"*.doc"
```

Note the differences between what is output in these three. Try the command **type** with the same arguments as you did for **dir** and note any differences.

To exit the script, enter **exit** for the command and just **<Return>** for the filename.

Altering the Loop Flow with break and continue

With **for** and **while** loops, you can terminate the loop prematurely with the **break** statement. The **break** makes the statement that follows the loop the next statement to be executed. For example:

124

```
for index in one two three
    do
    if [ $index = two ]
        then
        break
    fi
    echo $index
    done
```

will print out just

```
one
```

When the value of $index is two, the break statement is executed and the loop terminates.

You can use the continue statement to skip any remaining commands in the loop and start the next iteration. It goes to the end of the loop. An example is

```
for index in one two three
    do
    if [ $index = two ]
        then
        continue
    fi
    echo $index
    done
```

which will print out

```
one
three
```

When index is set to value of two, the test in the if statement is true and the continue is executed. This skips over the echo and continues the loop with the next value of the index (three).

case Statement

You may wish to perform one of a selection of commands, based on the value of a variable. The case statement provides a way of selecting a set of commands based on the value of a test string. Its syntax is

```
case test-string in
    pattern-1)
        commands
        ;;
    pattern-2)
        commands
        ;;
esac
```

The value of *test-string* is compared to *pattern-1*. If it matches, the *commands* listed up to the ;; are executed. If it does not match, *test-string* is compared to *pattern-2*. If it matches, the corresponding set of commands is executed. If no pattern matches *test-string*, no commands are executed.

For example, suppose you had a script called **case-script** with

```
case $1 in
    dir )
        echo String was dir
        ;;
    type )
        echo String was type
        ;;
    * )
        echo String was neither dir or type
        ;;
esac
```

If you executed **case-script** with

```
case-script dir
```

$1 would match the pattern **dir** and the output would be

```
String was dir
```

The patterns can include wildcards '*' and '?' and sets of characters such as [a-z]. Multiple patterns can be listed by separating them with a |. You can use * as the last pattern to operate on anything that was not matched by the previous patterns.

Workout case

1. This shell script interprets what looks like an MS-DOS command and executes the appropriate UNIX command. Enter it in a file called **ms-dos-loop-1**.

```
#! /bin/sh
not-done=1
while [ $not-done = 1 ]
do
      echo Enter command
      read command
      echo Enter filename
      read filename
      case $command in
          [Dd][Ii][Rr] )
                echo Directory of $filename
                ls -l $filename
                ;;
          [Tt][Yy][Pp][Ee] )
                echo Listing of $filename
                cat $filename
                ;;
          [Ee][Xx][Ii][Tt] )
                not-done=0
                ;;
          * )
                echo Unknown Command $command
                ;;
      esac
done
```

2. Run this command as

```
ms-dos-loop-1
```

Try the commands DIR, dir, type and Type with one.doc as the filename.

To exit the script, enter exit for the command and just <Return> for the filename.

3. Run ms_dos_loop from the preceding workout.

Try the commands DIR, dir, type and Type with one.doc as the filename.

To exit the script, enter exit for the command and just <Return> for the filename. Note the difference between how ms-dos-loop and ms-dos-loop-1 work. The latter accepts any capitalization.

True and False

There are two programs named **true** and **false**. The sole purpose of these programs is to provide a true (0) and a false (nonzero) value as the exit code. The programs can be used as the test command for any of the control-flow statements.

Evaluating Expressions

The general-purpose expression evaluator **expr** is useful in shell scripts. It performs computations on the arguments that are passed to it and outputs the result. The arithmetic operators include +, -, *, and /. The logical operators are AND (&), OR (|), and NOT (!). It also has the ability for a regular expression matching (:). For example, if a script called **add** was

```
expr $1 + $2
```

and you typed

```
add 5 10
```

then **15** would be displayed on the output.

The **expr** command is typically used to put a computed value into a shell variable. Command substitution is commonly used with **expr**. For example, if you wanted to add one to the value of **$adder**, you would type

```
adder=`expr $adder + 1`
```

Strip Directory from Pathname

This command is useful in shell scripts to eliminate the directory portion of a filename that is passed to a script. The syntax is

```
basename string suffix
```

It outputs the *string* without any leading directory to the standard output. If you include *suffix*, that suffix is also striped from *string*. **basename** is usually used with backquotes to put the output value into a shell variable. For example,

```
name-no-directory=`basename $1`
```

removes the directory path from the value of **$1** and places it into **name-no-directory**.

Workout Shell script for **basename**

---

1. Enter the following script as **copy-ext**. The script copies all files with extension given by the first argument to files with the extension given by the second argument

```
#! /bin/sh
for name in *.$1
do
      cp $name `basename $name $1`$2
      done
```

2. Run the script as

```
$ copy-ext doc bak
```

3. Do a directory listing to see the new files.

```
$ ls
```

4. If you don't have any files that have a **doc** extension, you will get an error message from the script, when you run the **copy-ext-c** script. Try running it as:

```
$ copy-ext-c xxx bak
```

You could first count the number of matching files, with:

```
file-count=`ls | grep ".*\.$1' | wc -1`
if [ file-count -le 0 ]
    then
          echo No files with that extension
          exit 1
fi
```

Add these lines to the beginning of **copy-ext-c** and try running it again with:

```
$ copy-ext-c xxx bak
```

Variable Expansion

As we discussed in earlier chapters, if you surround a string with quotation marks, special shell characters are not interpreted. Quotations around the **$@** and **$*** variables cause them to have different values when passed to a command executed by a script. The value **"$*"** is a single quoted string. The value **"$@"** is a set of strings. For example, suppose that you had a script called **lister** containing just

```
lister-sub "$*"
lister-sub "$@"
```

The **lister-sub** script contains just

```
echo Number of parameters is $#
echo First parameter is $1
```

If you executed **lister** with

```
lister one two three
```

the output will be

```
Number of parameters is 1
First parameter is one two three
Number of parameters is 3
First parameter is one
```

The value of **"$*"** is **"one two three"**. The value of **"$@"** is **"one"** **"two"** **"three"**.

Interrupt Processing

If the user interrupts your shell script, you may want to perform certain commands. The **trap** statement allows you to specify commands to be performed if an interrupt occurs. The format is

```
trap command signals
```

The *signals* are integer values, which describe the type of interrupt. Common ones are 2 for user interrupt and 3 for user quit, generated by <control-C> and <control-\>. When a listed signal occurs, *command* is executed. For example, suppose that you create a temporary file with the name $temp in your script. The statement

```
trap 'rm $temp; exit 1' 2 3
```

will be executed if the user interrupts the script. The **rm** command will remove that temporary file and the script will exit with an unsuccessful code. It is usually a good idea for scripts to remove all temporary files regardless of whether it exits normally or by user interrupt.

Debugging Shell Scripts

You can run a shell script by running the shell and specifying the name of the script. If you do this, you can specify options on the line. The form is

```
sh options script-name
```

The options include verbose mode (**-v**) to print each line as it is read (before argument substitution) and **-x** to print each line as it is executed.

KORN SHELL

The Korn shell has the same syntax as the Bourne shell, but it has some useful additional features. These include the history feature, which is similar to DOSKEY and job control. The Korn shell is not as common as either the Bourne shell or the C shell, so just a few comments will be made here.

You can store a history of commands that you type by setting the size of the history with the **HISTSIZE** variable. The history between log-in sessions will be stored by setting a filename for the **HISTFILE** variable. You can recall earlier commands and edit them using **vi** features or another editor's features.

Your home directory can be specified by ~, rather than having to spell it out completely. You can assign aliases for commands, which work like fast shell scripts. Computation of variable expressions can be performed using the **let** statement rather than the **expr** program. Shell programmers will find a number of additional features, such as **select**.

Job control allows you to start and stop processes and to place processes into the background and recall them to the foreground. Job control is described in more detail in Chapter 11.

Further Exploration

If you want to explore further the capabilities of **sh**, you should look in the **man** pages with regard to "here documents" (**<<** symbol), **exec**, and conditional substitution of shell variables.

FOR FURTHER INFORMATION

Bourne, S. R. 1984. *An Introduction to the UNIX Shell*. UNIX Documentation Set.

Bolsky, M. I., and Korn, D. G. 1989. *The KornShell Command and Programming Language*. Englewood Cliffs, N.J.: Prentice Hall. Details on the Korn shell.

Kernighan, Brian W., and Pike, Rob. 1984. *The UNIX Programming Environment*. Englewood Cliffs, N.J.: Prentice-Hall. Programming the Bourne shell, **awk**, and other tools.

Rosenblatt, Bill. 1993. *Learning the Korn Shell*. O'Reilly.

COMMAND SUMMARY

Shell variables
Setting	*name*=*value*
Resetting	*name*=
Printing	**set**
Exporting to environment	**export** *name*
Primary prompt	**$PS1**
Secondary prompt	**$PS2**
Exit status of last command	**$?**
Pid of last background command	**$!**
Pid of the current shell	**$$**

Script variables
Arguments	**$***number*
Number of arguments	**$#**
List of arguments	**$@** and **$***
Shifting arguments	**shift**
Reading variables	**read** *variable(s)*
Login script	**.profile**
Execute in current shell	**.** *script-name*

Evaluate expressions	`expr` *expression*
Strip directory from pathname	`basename` *string*
True always	`true`
False always	`false`
Trap interrupts	`trap` *commands signals*
Control flow	

Control flow

if statement
```
if test-command
    then
      commands
fi
if test-command
    then
      commands
    else
      commands
fi
elif
```

exit
```
exit value
```

for
```
for index in list
    do
      commands
    done
for index
    do
      commands
    done
```

while
```
while test-command
    do
      statements
    done
```

until
```
until test-command
    do
      statements
    done
```

break
```
break
```

continue
```
continue
```

case
```
case test-string in
pattern-1)
      commands
      ;;
pattern-2)
      commands
      ;;
esac
```

Debugging shell scripts	`sh` *options* `script-name`
Verbose mode	`-v`
Executed lines	`-x`
Test program	
see Table 10–1	

11 | C SHELL

Tell me what I just did

The C shell has become a popular shell, although it is not available on all UNIX systems. It has a history mechanism, job control, and a syntax for script files that is similar to the C language syntax.

C SHELL USAGE

The default prompt for the C shell is **%**. If **csh** is specified in the **/etc/passwd** file as your log-in shell, you will get this prompt. You can change this by setting the **prompt** variable. The standard shell processing described in Chapter 8 applies to the C shell. If you have an error such as unmatched quotation marks, the shell will complain with a message.

A number of parameters can be set for the C shell to change its behavior. One of the most common is **set ignoreeof**, which eliminates being able to exit from the shell with <control-D>. You must type **logout** instead. This prevents premature logging out by typing one <control-D> too many.

The **.login** file is executed by the shell the first time you log in. The **.logout** file is executed when you log out. The **.cshrc** file is executed by the shell every time it is started. You can put settings into **.cshrc** for shell variables you want to set in every shell process that is created, such as with the **( )** subshell operators.

To execute a shell script in the same process as the current shell, use the **source** statement, as

```
source script-file
```

This is useful if *script-file* contains settings for shell variables. For example, to test out a new **.login** file without logging off, you would type

```
source .login
```

If you typed

```
.login
```

a new child process would be created. Any changes in the shell or environment variable would be made in that process. When it exits, the changes would not be reflected back into the parent process.

When writing C shell scripts, you should include a comment on the first line in the form

```
#! /bin/csh
```

If the script is run by another type of shell, that shell will spawn a **csh** to execute the script. This is necessary since the syntax for control flow is different between shells.

History

The history mechanism saves commands for later recall, much like the DOSKEY feature in MS-DOS. To turn on history, set a value for **history** as

```
set history = number
```

To see the history, type

```
history
```

To reexecute a previous command, you use **!** followed by an indication of which command. To perform the immediately preceding command, use **!!**. To execute a numbered command on the history list, use **!** *number*. To perform a command containing particular characters, use **!** *string*. The most recent command that contains *string* will be executed. You can modify the event that is recalled by adding :s/*old-string*/*new-string* to any of these commands. This substitutes *new-string* for *old-string*. There are some additional command modifiers, which are listed in the **man** pages for **csh**.

To save history between log-in sessions, enter

set savehist = *number*

The *number* is the number of past commands that will be remembered.

Alias

An alias is a short name for a longer command. Using an alias is similar to using a shell script. The difference is that an alias will be substituted wherever its name occurs. The syntax for creating an alias is

alias *name command*

An example is

alias dir ls -l

Whenever you type **dir** or wherever you use it in a script, **ls -l** will be substituted. An alias is useful to manipulate arguments using history, as the substitutions will be made when you edit a command.

Job Control

Processes are grouped into jobs, which are a collection of one or more processes. An example of a job is the group of processes created when a pipe is run (e.g., **cat one.doc | sort**). A job is run in either the foreground or the background. A foreground job has the ability to read from a terminal. A background job cannot. Only one job can be the foreground job at any time.

Using job control, you can alter the status of your jobs. You place a job into the background by using **&** at the end of the command line. Alternatively, you can stop a foreground job with <control-Z> and put it into background by typing **bg**. Regardless of which method you use, a number will be printed out that identifies the job. This job number is not the same as the process id. The job number corresponds to a group of process ids.

The **jobs** command lists the currently active jobs. Each job has the job number listed with it. You can bring a background job to the foreground so that it can read from the terminal with **fg** command. You need to specify the job number as

fg %*job-number*

As a shortcut, you can type

%*job-number*

You can also identify a job with a string as

fg %*string*

This form brings to the foreground the job with the *string* in the command used to start the job.

The output of background jobs will be intermixed with foreground jobs. You can execute **stty tostop** to make background jobs stop if they attempt to output to the terminal. When you bring a job to the foreground, it will start outputting again. The C shell notifies you when a job changes state (e.g., when it stops or it completes). This notification occurs only at the next C shell prompt, unless you set **notify**.

Workout Job control

---

1. Start **vi**.

   ```
   $ vi one.doc
   ```

2. Stop it with **<control-Z>**

   The system will respond with

   ```
   Stopped
   ```

   Put into background with **bg**

3. Start up **find**

   ```
   $ find / -name "sam" -print
   ```

4. Stop it with **<control-Z>**

   The system will respond with

```
Stopped
```

Put into background with **bg**

5. In order to stop the output of **find**, type

   ```
   $ stty tostop
   ```

6. Find out the current jobs

   ```
   $ jobs
   ... (list of jobs)
   ```

7. Pick out the one that is **vi**. Then use

   ```
   $ fg %job-number-of-vi
   ```

8. Quit **vi** with

   ```
   :q!
   ```

9. Bring back up **find** with

   ```
   $ fg %job-number-of-find
   ```

10. Stop the program with

    ```
    <control-C>
    ```

DIAGRAM Processes for this Workout

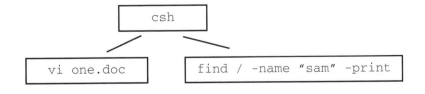

Filename Shortcuts

Your home directory can be abbreviated using ~. If you had a directory called **bin** in your home directory, you could refer to this as **~/bin** instead of using the full pathname.

Most versions of the C shell have a filename completion mode. This is enabled by setting the **filec** variable. When you type a partial filename, followed by <Escape>, the shell will complete the filename if there is a single match. If there are multiple matches, it will not make a completion. In that case, you type <control-D> to get a list of matching filenames, then enter what is necessary to get a single match.

You can turn off filename expansion (of the '*', '?', and "[..]" characters) by **set noglob**. This might be useful if you use filename matching characters frequently in commands. The variable is called **noglob** because the filename matching is sometimes referred to as "globbing".

Redirection

You may want to redirect the standard error output, as well as the standard output. The form

```
command >& filename
```

redirects both the standard error and standard outputs to *filename*. The |& symbol redirects both outputs for a pipe. If you only want to redirect the standard error output, you will need to use

```
(command > output-file) >& error-file
```

The standard output inside the parentheses is directed to *output-file*. The standard error output is directed to *error-file*.

When the output is redirected to a file and the file already exists, the file will be overwritten. To prevent this from happening, you can set **noclobber**. If this is set and the file exists, an error message is issued.

VARIABLES

As shown previously, the variables are set in the C shell by using the **set** command. The syntax is

```
set name = value
```

Some variables are switches—they are either on or off. You can set a variable on by typing

    set *name*

To turn a variable off or to remove it from the list, you use **unset**, as

    unset *name*

To print out the values of all the shell variables, type **set**.
  Standard C shell variables include the following:

$user	Username
$path	Current path
$home	Home directory
$shell	Current shell
$term	Terminal type
$status	Last command exit status
$noclobber	Avoids overwriting an existing file when using redirection
$nonomatch	Avoids "No match" message if no filename match
$ignoreeof	Prevents logout with <control-D>

The **nonomatch** variable turns off reporting that a filename pattern had no matches. For example, you would see the following responses to the commands:

```
$ echo *.xxx
echo : No match
$ set nonomatch
$ echo *.xxx
$
```

If you specify a name for which there is no shell variable, the C shell looks in the environment variables to see if there is a matching name. If so, it uses that value.
  To set environment variables, you use the **setenv** command, as

    setenv *name value*

Note that there is no equals sign as for **set**. For example,

    setenv TO-BE-EXPORTED "this is a test"

The shell automatically exports and imports the values of **path**, **term**, and **shell** to and from the environment variables **PATH**, **TERM** , and **SHELL**.

To delete an environmental variable, use **unsetenv**. For example, to eliminate the preceding variable, use

```
unsetenv TO-BE-EXPORTED
```

We note for advanced programmers that you can have arrays of variables in the C shell. The syntax for setting an array is

```
set name = (value-1 value-2 value-3 ... )
```

The entire array is referred to as $name. Each element in the array is referred to with $name[index].

Shell Variables within a Script

The variables that are passed to shell scripts can be referred to with $1, $2, and so on. Alternatively, you can use $argv[1], $argv[2], and so on. This is the array syntax using **argv** as the name of the array. The number of arguments passed to the script is $#argv. The variable that contains all of the arguments is $argv[*] or $*.[1] The name used to invoke the shell script is $argv[0] or ${0}.

You can use the **shift** command to shift the values of the parameters in the **argv** array. This works like the MS-DOS SHIFT command. The value of $argv[1] ($1) takes on the value of $argv[2] ($2) g takes on the value of $argv[3] ($3), and so on. The value of $#argv is decremented by one each time you shift.

Reading Variables from Standard Input

Inside a script, you may need to input values from the user. You can get input from the keyboard with the $< operation. It is typically used as

```
set variable = $<
```

For example, if you had

```
echo "Enter a filename "
set name = $<
```

---

[1] You can also refer to all the arguments with $argv, since that is the name of the array.

the user would see

```
Enter a filename
```

If the response were **abc<Return>**, **name** would be set to **abc**.

Numerical Computations

You perform numerical computations with the **@** statement. This sets a numerical variable to the results of a computation. Its most common syntax is [2]

```
@ variable-name = expression
```

The *expression* can contain a combination of constants, variables, and operators. The expression operators include arithmetic, relational, and logical operators, as shown in Table 11-1. The equality and nonequality operators can apply to strings as well as to numerical values.

Be sure to include spaces around all these operators. Otherwise the operator will be considered as part of the preceding name or value. You will get error messages from the shell that it cannot understand your syntax.

CONTROL STATEMENTS

As mentioned earlier, MS-DOS has several control statements for use in scripts. We cover the C shell control statements here.

if Statement

The **if** statement tests to see if a condition is true or false. If it is true, it executes the command that follows. The syntax is

```
if ( test-condition ) command
```

The *test-condition* can be any expression that yields a logical value, with operators as listed in Table 11–1, such as

```
if ( $argv[1] == "dir" ) echo First parameter is dir
```

---

[2] The assignment operator can be replaced with **+=**, **-=**, ***=**, and **/=**, as known by C programmers.

TABLE 11–1 Expression Operators

Logical operators	
Equality	`==`
Not equal	`!=`
Greater than	`>`
Less than	`<`
Greater than or equal to	`>=`
Less than or equal to	`<=`
Boolean operators	
And	`&&`
Or	`||`
Not	`!`
Mathematical operators	
Add	`+`
Subtract	`-`
Multiply	`*`
Divide	`/`
Increment by 1	`++` [3]
Decrement by 1	`--` [3]
Modulo	`%`
Bitwise operators	
Shift right by bits	`>>`
Shift left by bits	`<<`
Bitwise one's complement	`~`
Bitwise inclusive or	`|`
Bitwise exclusive or	`^` [3]
Bitwise and	`&`

[3] Some versions do not have these tests.

A number of file tests are listed in Table 11–2. These tests can be applied to a filename. For example,

```
if ( -r one.doc ) echo $argv[1] is readable
```

executes the **echo** command if **one.doc** is readable.

You can test the exit code of a command by enclosing it in braces (**{** and **}**). You will need to include extra spaces so that the shell can interpret this properly. For example,

TABLE 11–2 File Tests

Test if file is a directory	`-d`
Test if file exists	`-e`
Test if file is ASCII (plain file)	`-f`
Test if executor is owner of file	`-o`
Test if file is readable	`-r`
Test if file is writable	`-w`
Test if file is executable	`-x`
Test if file is empty	`-z`

```
if ( { cmp -s one.doc two.doc } ) echo The two files are same
```

will execute the **echo** if **cmp** returns a true value (exit code of zero). The parentheses may be omitted when using the braces on many version of **csh**, so you could write this as:

```
if { cmp -s one.doc two.doc } echo The two files are same
```

You can test the exit code of the previous command by using **$status**. The previous example could be written as

```
cmp -s one.doc two.doc
if ( $status == 0 ) echo The two files are same
```

There is a form of the **if** statement that performs multiple commands if the test is true. Following the syntax for a set of commands:

```
if ( test-condition ) then
    commands
endif
```

The **then** must appear on the same line as the **if**. The example above could have been written as

```
cmp -s one.doc two.doc
if ( $status == 0 ) then
    echo The two files are same
endif
```
If you want to perform alternative commands, the syntax is

Workout Making a backup copy with editing

1. Enter the following script as **editor-c**.

```
#! /bin/csh
if ( -e $argv[1] ) then
    cp $argv[1] $argv[1].bak
endif
vi $argv[1]
```

Remember to **chmod u+x editor-c** so that you can run this script.

2. Try running this on **presidents**.

```
$ editor-c presidents
```

After you are finished editing, list the directory and note what is new with

```
$ ls p*
```

```
if ( test-condition ) then
    commands-if-true
else
    commands-if-false
endif
```

For example,

```
if ( -r $argv[1] ) then
    echo $argv[1] is readable
else
    echo $argv[1] is not readable
endif
```

will echo the appropriate response.

To form a set of tests, you can use the `else if`. The form is

```
if ( test-condition ) then
    commands-if-true
else if ( test-condition-2 ) then
    commands-if-2-true
else
    commands-if-both-false
endif
```

You can use as many `else if` statements as necessary; for example,

```
if ( { cmp -s one.doc two.doc } ) then
    echo one.doc and two.doc match
else if ( { cmp -s one.doc three.doc } ) then
    echo one.doc and three.doc match
else if ( { cmp -s two.doc three.doc } ) then
    echo two.doc and three.doc match
endif
```

The first time that **cmp** returns true, the appropriate response is output.

Exit with a Value

The **exit** statement terminates the script and returns the value that follows it as the exit code. The syntax is

```
exit value
```

A proper script should be terminated with an **exit** and a value. If it terminates by reaching the end of the file, the value it returns may vary every time it executes.

Workout `if`

1. This shell script interprets MS-DOS commands and executes the appropriate UNIX command. Enter in a file called **ms-dos-c**.

```
#! /bin/csh
set nonomatch
if ( $#argv < 2) then
```

```
            echo Usage: ms-dos command filename
            exit 1
      endif
      if ( $argv[1] == "dir" ) then
            echo Directory of $argv[2]
            ls -l $argv[2]
      else if ( $argv[1] == "type" ) then
            echo Listing of $argv[2]
            cat $argv[2]
      else
            echo Unknown command $argv[1]
      endif
```

2. Run this command as

```
$ ms-dos-c dir one.doc
$ ms-dos-c dir *.doc
$ ms-dos-c dir "*.doc"
$ ms-dos-c type one.doc
```

Note the differences between what is output in these four operations.

Looping on a List

The **foreach** loops through a given list of values, much like the FOR statement in MS-DOS. The syntax is

```
foreach index-variable ( value-list )
      commands
      end
```

The *index-variable* takes on each successive value in *value-list* every time around the loop. The *commands* are then executed for that value of *index-variable*; for example,

```
foreach name ( one.doc two.doc three.doc )
      echo File is $name
      cat $name
      end
```

The **foreach** loop will be executed three times. The first time, the value of **$name** will be **one.doc**; the second time, **two.doc**; and the third time, **three.doc**.

You can specify a filename matching pattern in the *value-list*, such as

```
foreach name ( *.doc )
    echo File is $name
    cat $name
    end
```

You can loop over all the input arguments with **$argv** [*] as

```
foreach name ( $argv[*] )
    echo File is $name
    cat $name
    end
```

If the script containing these lines were named **for-script** and was executed as

```
for-script one.doc two.doc three.doc
```

the loop would be executed three times, once for each argument.

Workout foreach

---

1. Write a script, call it **exists-c** that determines if a set of files exists. It could look like

```
#! /bin/csh
foreach name ( $argv[*] )
    if ( -e $name ) then
        echo $name exists
    else
        echo $name does not exist
    endif
    end
```

2. Try it out with

```
$ exists-c one.doc two.doc xxxx
```

Looping with `while`

You can execute a number of commands repeatedly with the **`while`** statement. The syntax is

```
while ( test-condition )
    commands
end
```

If *test-condition* is true, the *commands* are executed. The *test-condition* is tested again and if it is still true, the loop is reexecuted: for example,

```
set name = anything
while ( $name != "" )
    echo Enter filename to type
    set name = $<
    if ( $name != "") cat $name
    end
```

This script will loop, each time asking for a filename to pass to **cat**. If the user just enters <Return>, **$name** will have no characters in it. The loop will exit since **$name != ""** will be false.

Workout `while`

---

1. This shell script interprets MS-DOS commands and executes the appropriate UNIX command. Enter in a file called **ms-dos-loop-c**.

```
#! /bin/csh
set nonomatch
set not-done = 1
while ( $not-done == 1 )
    echo Enter command
    set command = $<
    echo Enter filename
    set filename = $<
    if ( $command == "dir" ) then
        echo Directory $filename
        ls -l $filename
```

```
        else if ( $command == "type" ) then
            echo Listing of $filename
            cat $filename
        else if ( $command == "exit" ) then
            set not-done = 0
        else
            echo Unknown command $command
        endif
    end
```

2. Run this command as

```
ms-dos-loop-c
```

Try the command **dir** three times and use the following as file-names:

```
one.doc
*.doc
"*.doc"
```

Note the differences between what is output in these three. Try the command **type** with the same arguments as you did for **dir** and note any differences.

To exit the script, enter **exit** for the command and enter just `<Return>` for the filename.

Altering the Loop Flow with break and continue

With the **foreach** and the **while** statements, you can terminate the loop early with the **break** statement. It goes to the statement that follows the loop. For example,

```
foreach index ( one two three )
    if ( $index == two ) break
    echo $index
    end
```

will print out just

```
one
```

You can use the **continue** statement to skip any commands in the loop and start the next iteration. It goes to the end of the loop. An example with the **continue** is

```
foreach index ( one two three )
    if ( $index == two ) continue
    echo $index
    end
```

This will print out

```
one
three
```

When **index** is set to value of **two**, the **if** statement test is true and the **continue** is executed. This skips over the **echo** and continues the loop with the next value of the index (**three**).

Selection

You can select among a number of different alternative commands using the **switch** statement. The syntax is

```
switch(string)
case pattern-1:
    commands-1
    breaksw
case pattern-2:
    commands-2
    breaksw

        . . .
default:
    commands-default
    breaksw
endsw
```

If *string* matches *pattern-1*, *commands-1* are executed. The **breaksw** terminates the command list. If *string* matches *pattern-2*, *commands-2* are executed. The statements following the optional **default:** label are executed if none of the patterns are matched. The patterns can include wildcards (as '*', '?') and sets of characters as **[a-z]**; for example,

```
switch ($argv[1])
case time :
    echo String was time
    breaksw
case date :
    echo String was date
    breaksw
default:
    echo String was neither date or time
endsw
```

If you executed a script with this **switch** in it as

```
test-script time
```

$argv[1] would match the pattern **time** and the output would be

```
String was time
```

Workout switch

1. This shell script interprets MS-DOS commands and executes the appropriate UNIX command. Enter in a file called **ms-dos-loop-1-c**.

```
#! /bin/csh
set nonomatch
set not-done = 1
while ( $not-done == 1 )
    echo Enter command
    set command = $<
    echo Enter filename
    set filename = $<
    switch($command)
    case [Dd][Ii][Rr]:
        echo Directory of $filename
        ls $filename
        breaksw
    case [Tt][Yy][Pp][Ee]:
        echo Listing of $filename
```

```
            cat $filename
            breaksw
    case [Ee] [Xx] [Ii] [Tt] :
            set not-done = 0
            breaksw
    default:
            echo Did not understand $command
            breaksw
    endsw
    end
```

2. Run this command as

   `ms-dos-loop-1-c`

   Try the commands **DIR**, **dir**, **type** and **Type** with **one.doc** as the filename.

   To exit the script, enter **exit** for the command and just **<Return>** for the filename.

3. Run **ms-dos-loop** from the preceding workout.

   Try the commands **DIR**, **dir**, **type** and **Type** with **one.doc** as the filename.

   To exit the script, enter **exit** for the command and just **<Return>** for the filename.

   Note the difference between how **ms-dos-loop-c** and **ms-dos-loop-1-c** work. The latter accepts any capitalization.

Transferring Control

The **goto** statement transfers control to another statement in the script. The syntax is

```
goto label
...
label:
```

The *label* precedes the statement to which control is to be transferred: for example,

```
if ( $#argv == 3 ) goto okay
echo "You need three arguments"
exit 1
okay:
...
```

You can usually use the other control statements to perform the same logic as the `goto`.

Filename Parts

You can break a variable that is a filename into parts using filename modifiers. These modifiers choose the directory portion (`:h`), the nondirectory portion (`:t`), everything before a period (`:r`), or everything after a period (`:e`). For example,

```
set name = /usr/home/george/file.doc
echo $name:h
echo $name:t
echo $name:r
echo $name:e
```

will output

```
/user/home/george
file.doc
/usr/home/george/file
doc
```

Workout Filename parts

---

1. Enter the following script as **copy-ext-c**. The script copies all files with extension given by the first argument to files with the extension given by the second argument.

```
#! /bin/csh
foreach name ( *.$argv[1] )
    cp $name $name:r.$argv[2]
    end
```

2. Run the script as

```
$ copy-ext-c doc bak
```

3. Do a directory listing to see the new files

```
$ ls
```

4. If you don't have any files that have a **doc** extension, you will get an error message from the **script**, when you run the **copy-ext-c** script. Try running it as:

```
$ copy-ext-c xxx bak
```

You could first count the number of matching files, with:

```
set nonomatch
set file-count = `ls | grep ".*\.$argv[1]' | wc -
1`
if ( $file-count <= 0 ) exit 1
```

Add those lines to the beginning of **copy-ext-c** and try running it again with:

```
$ copy-ext-c xxx bak
```

Interrupt Processing

If the user interrupts your shell script, you may want to perform certain commands. The **onintr** statement allows you to specify what statement to execute if the interrupt key (<control-C>) is pressed. The syntax is

```
onintr label
```

When the interrupt occurs, the next statement to be executed is that which follows *label:*. For example, if you create temporary files with the name **$temp** in your script, you may wish to have

```
onintr complete
...
complete:
```

```
rm $temp
exit 1
```

The **rm** command will be executed if the user interrupts the script. It will remove that temporary file and the script will exit with an unsuccessful code. It is usually a good idea for a script to remove all temporary files regardless of whether it exits normally or by user interrupt.

Debugging Shell Scripts

You can run a shell script by running the shell and specifying the name of the script. If you do this, you can specify options on the line. The form is

```
csh options script-name
```

The options include verbose mode (**-v**) to print each line as it is read (before argument substitution) and **-x** to print each line as it is executed.

FOR FURTHER INFORMATION

The **man** pages for **csh** lists a number of additional features. One is the **eval** statement, which takes a string, converts it into an argument list, and causes the string to be interpreted by the shell. Another is the directory stack (**dirs**, **pushd**, **popd**), which is useful for going back to a previous directory. You may also wish to examine arrays of shell variables in more detail.

Anderson, Gail, and Anderson, Paul. 1986. *The UNIX C Shell Field Guide.* Englewood Cliffs, N.J.: Prentice Hall.
Arick, Martin R. 1992. *UNIX C Shell Desk Reference.* Fort Bragg, Calif.: QED.
Joy, W. 1984. *An Introduction to the C Shell.* UNIX Documentation Set.

COMMAND SUMMARY

Logging out	`logout`
Log-in script	`.login`
Log-out script	`.logout`
Shell startup script	`.cshrc`
Executing in same shell	`source script-file`

History
   Setting size   `set history` = *number*
                                     `set savehist` = *number*
   Listing   `history`
   Recalling previous   `!!`
   Recalling particular   `!`*number*
                                       `!`*string*
   Editing command   `:s/`*old-string*`/`*new-string*
Setting alias   `alias` *name command*
Job control
   Placing in background   `&`
   Stop and place current in
      background   `<control-Z>` and `bg`
   Listing   `jobs`
   Bring to foreground   `fg %`*job-number*
                                       `fg %`*string*
                                       `%`*job-number*

Filename shortcuts
   Home directory   `~`
   Filename completion   `set filec`
   No filename matching   `set noglob`
Filename parts
   Directory portion   `:h`
   Nondirectory portion   `:t`
   Before a period   `:r`
   After a period   `:e`
Redirecting standard error
   To file   `>&`
   In pipe   `|&`
Variables
   Setting shell variables   `set` *name* = *value*
                                       `set` *name*
   Unsetting variables   `unset` *name*
   Printing values   `set`
   Environment variables   `setenv` *name value*
Shell variables
   Prompt   `$prompt`
   Ignore eof to log out   `$ignoreeof`
   Avoids overwriting an
      existing file when using   `$noclobber`
      redirection
   User name   `$user`
   Current path   `$path`
   Home directory   `$home`

Terminal type	`$term`
Last command exit status	`$status`
Avoid "No match" message if no filename match	`$nonomatch`
Script variables	
Arguments	`$argv[`*number*`]` or `$`*number*
Number of arguments	`$#argv`
All arguments	`$argv[*]`
Name of script	`$argv[0]`
Shift variables	`shift`
Reading from standard input	`$<`
Comments	`#`
Numeric computations	`@` *variable-name* `=` *expression*
Operators—see Table 11–1	
Control statements	
if	`if (` *test-condition* `)` *command*

	`if (` *test-condition* `) then`
	   commands
	`endif`

	`if (` *test-condition* `) then`
	   commands-if-true
	`else`
	   commands-if-false
	`endif`

	`if (` *test-condition* `) then`
	   commands-if-true
	`else if (` *test-condition-2* `)`
	   `then`
	   commands-if-2-true
	`else`
	   commands-if-both-false
	`endif`

Exit with a value	`exit` *value*

Looping on list	`foreach` *index-variable* `(` *value-list* `)`
	   commands
	`end`

Looping with `while`	`while (` *test-condition* `)`
	   commands
	`end`

Break	`break`
Continue	`continue`

| Selection | ```
switch(string)
case pattern-1:
    commands-1
    breaksw
case pattern-2:
    commands-2
    breaksw

    ...
default:
    commands-default
    breaksw
endsw
``` |
| Goto | ```
goto label
...
label:
``` |
Interrupt processing	`onintr label`
Debugging shell scripts	`csh options script-name`
Verbose mode	`-v`
Executed lines	`-x`

12 | SYSTEM ADMINISTRATION

Somebody's gotta know what's going on

You may be the only user on your UNIX system. In that case you will be the administrator. The administrator takes care of backing up files, establishing new accounts, and other administrative chores. Even if you are not the administrator, some knowledge of the administrative functions may be useful.

THE SUPERUSER

Because the administrator needs to be able to copy everyone's files and to maintain system files, he/she is given extraordinary privileges. This user is known as the superuser. The name of this user is "root" and the numerical user id is zero. An ordinary user may become a superuser by typing the command **su** and entering the password for "root". The prompt for superuser is set to **#**. One exits superuser mode by typing **<control-D>**.

THE ADMINISTRATIVE DIRECTORY

The **/etc** directory contains most of the programs and files that are of interest to the administrator. For example, the list of users and their passwords is kept in **/etc/passwd**.

161

USERS AND GROUPS

Adding Users

A few steps are necessary to add a user to your system. Usually, the system has an **/etc/adduser** script, which simplifies the job. If it does, follow the instructions for it. If it does not, you will need to add the user manually.

The first step is to add an entry in password file **/etc/passwd**. You use either **vi** on System V or **vipw** on BSD. Each line of the password file consists of

```
login-name : password : user-id : group-id:
   information :  home-directory : program-to-start
```

Login-name is the name used at the "login:" prompt. It is also referred to as the "user name". It should be unique to all other login-names. The *password* field is an encrypted version of the user's password. The *user-id* is a numerical value that represents the user. It is possible for two different login-names to have the same *user-id*. The user-id is what determines the file permissions, not the login-name. Normally, each login-name has a unique user-id. The *group-id* is the number of the group to which the user belongs. This should correspond to an entry in **/etc/groups**. The *information* field contains any useful comments, such as the real name of the user. The *home-directory* is the home directory for the user. The *program-to-start* is the program that will be run when the user logs in successfully . This program is normally a shell, such as **/bin/sh** or **/bin/csh**. However, it can be any program. Once this program exits, the user will be logged off.

A typical entry to add might read

```
kpugh:7ahq2f:42:20:Ken Pugh:/usr/users/kpugh:/bin/sh
```

The password in **/etc/passwd** is encrypted. Even as superuser, you cannot decrypt it. If the password field is empty, no password is required. To set the initial password for a user, you use the **passwd** program. You can also use this program if a user forgets his/her password. To change the password for a user, type

```
passwd login-name
```

You will be prompted for the new password and for reconfirmation of the password.

The home directory for the user needs to be created. Typically, this is a directory in **/usr** or **/usr/users**, but you can put it anywhere. To create the home directory, type the following, with the necessary substitutions:

```
mkdir home-directory
chown home-directory user-name
chgrp home-directory user-group
chmod u+rwx home-directory
```

The final step is to copy any standard shell log-in files to the user's home directory. The files should include at least commands that set the PATH, TERM, and MAIL variables. The user may modify these after logging on. The log-in file is either **.profile** or **.login**, depending on whether the shell is Bourne or C.

Deleting a User

The steps for deleting a user follow the ones for adding one. You should edit **/etc/passwd** and place a "*****" in the password field. No valid password can encrypt to this value, so that the user will be unable to log-in. Alternatively, you may change the startup program to a program that notifies the user that the account is no longer active. You should not get rid of the user immediately as some accounting programs require the information contained on the user line.

You then backup the user's home directory (and all subdirectories) to tape or diskette. The tape archiving program (**tar**) is useful for doing this and is described in Chapter 16. Then remove all the user's files and directories with

```
rm -rf home-directory
```

This removes all the files starting in the *home-directory* and all subdirectories (**-r** for recursive) and does not ask for confirmation to delete read-only files (**-f**). Be careful. Do not run this command using a needed directory as the *home-directory*. For example, if you use **/** as the *home-directory*, you will wipe out your entire system.

Groups

Each user is a member of one or more groups. The id of the primary group is listed in **/etc/passwd**. The groups are listed in **/etc/group**. Each line gives the information for one group and has the format

```
name: password : group-id : login-name-list
```

The *name* field is the name of the group. The *password* field is not normally used and is set to "*". [1] The numeric *group-id* identifies the group for permission purposes. The *login-name-list* lists the log-in ids for the members of the group, separated by commas.

To add a new group, add a new line to this file, following the above format. To add a new user to a group, add the log-in name to the list for that group.

Communicating with Your Users

There are a number of ways to communicate with your users, depending on the urgency of the message. The most immediate is to write to all users with **wall**. This works like **write**, but implicitly uses the list of current log-ins as the "send to" list: for example,

```
wall System will be going down in five minutes
```

The message of the day file can be changed to reflect current operating system status. This file is printed out whenever a user logs in. The message file is **/etc/motd**. You might have something in this file like

```
The system will be shut down between 2 and 3 a.m.
```

Some systems also support the concept of news. News is kept in **/usr/msgs** on BSD and **/usr/news** on System V. Running **msgs** (BSD) or **news** (System V) displays new messages that have not yet been seen by the user. This is useful only if all users have a call to the program in their log-in file.

---

[1] The password field was included originally so that nongroup members could become a group member by entering the password. It turned out that this feature could introduce holes in the security system.

Workout Administrator

1. Add a new user, using either a system script or manually, as given before.
2. Log in as that user, and add a few files to the user's directory.
3. Log in as superuser and remove the user, per the instructions given above.

DISK ORGANIZATION

Mounted Partitions

MS-DOS uses a different drive letter (e.g., C:, D:) for a separate physical disk drive, such as a floppy or a hard disk. In addition, a drive letter may be assigned to each partition on the hard disk. Each drive has its own root (\) directory. UNIX uses a different organization. There is one file system that contains the root / directory. The other disk partitions are "mounted" as directories of this root system.

The physical partitions for your hard disk are set when UNIX is installed. Similar to the MS-DOS FORMAT command, the UNIX **mkfs** (make file system) command formats a partition and installs a root directory on it. This command is run on each partition when the system is installed. The characteristics of each partition may be stored on the disk itself or in a table in **/etc/disktab**, depending on the version of UNIX.

To access a partition from your root file system, the **mount** command is used. This is similar to the MS-DOS JOIN command. The syntax is

> **mount** *partition-device directory*

The *partition-device* is the name of the partition, usually something like **/dev/fh0g**. The *directory* is the name of a directory on which to mount the partition.[2] The root directory of the partition is then accessible by referring to the name of *directory*. For example, if you typed

> **mount /dev/fh0g /tmp**

the root directory of the partition **/dev/fh0g** is accessible by the name **/tmp**. If there were a file named **something** in the root directory of **/dev/fh0g**, you would access it as **/tmp/something**.

---

[2] **mount** can be used to automatically mount entries in **/etc/fstab**. Check the **man** pages for details.

Diagram of mount example **mount/dev/fh0g /tmp**

Root device	Another device with a file system **/dev/fh0g**
/(root)	/(root)
/	/
tmp <==>	something

Once a partition or other file system type [3] is mounted, it looks to the user as if it is part of the normal file system. When a file system is mounted, an entry is made in a file of mounted file systems (`/etc/mnttab` on System V or `/etc/mtab` on BSD). You can list this file by typing `mount` with no parameters. To remove a file system, the `umount` command and the name of the partition and/or directory are used. For example,

```
umount /dev/fh0g
```

or

```
umount /tmp
```

removes the file system mounted with the previous command.

The `mount` commands are usually set up as part of your startup procedure.

Disk Usage per File System

Just as in MS-DOS, there is a limit to how much information can be stored on the hard disk. The disk free command `df` shows the number of free blocks left on the file system. Each block contains either 512 or 1024 bytes. `df` gives a percentage of the disk that is used. This percentage may be greater than 100 percent. The design of the file system is such that if the actual percentage utilized is greater than about 90 percent, the disk block allocation scheme becomes too fragmented. The percentage shown on the output is based on about 90 percent of the blocks.

Disk Usage per Directory

The disk usage (`du`) command reports the number of blocks used by the files in a directory and every subdirectory. It can print the number of blocks for each file with the `-a` option. Running `du` can determine which directories are using up a lot of space on a file system.

Core Files

When a process terminates abnormally, images of the process are saved to disk to a file named **core**. The file will be stored in the current directory. These core files tend to be fairly large. Programmers can use

---

[3] Network File System (NFS) is a common type of file system that is mounted. Its description is beyond the scope of this book.

debugging tools to examine them to determine the cause of the termination. Regular users have no need for them. To get rid of old **core** files, such as ones that have not been accessed for a week, you can run **find** with

```
find / -name core -atime +7 -exec rm {} \;
```

Workout Disk usage

---

1. Check out the amount of space your system has and see which directories are using it.

```
$ df
$ du / | more
```

2. Find out if there are any core files on your system.

```
find / -name core -print
```

File Checking

The MS-DOS CHKDSK program verifies the integrity of the file system. It checks to see if the File Allocation Table (FAT) is consistent. It will also create files for disk blocks that are assumed to be allocated but which do not appear in a directory.

The UNIX file system checking program **fsck** performs similar operations. It checks to see if each nonfree inode (file information node) is listed in at least one directory. If not, it puts an entry for the inode in the directory **lost+found**. It also checks to see if the free block list corresponds to the blocks that are not allocated for files. If there are unlisted blocks that are not allocated, they are placed in the free block list. Unlike MS-DOS, there is no way to recover a deleted file in UNIX. As soon as a file is deleted, all disk blocks used for that file are marked as free.

The **fsck** program uses the file **/etc/fstab** (BSD) or **/etc/checklist** (System V) to determine which file systems to check. The syntax for **/etc/fstab** is

name mount-point read-write dump-time checking-order

The *name* is the name of the device. The *mount-point* is the directory on which is has been mounted. The *read-write* field states whether it has been mounted in read/write or read-only mode. The *dump-time* indicates the frequency of backup. The *checking-order* is a numerical value that describes the order in which the files will be checked by **fsck**. The /etc/checklist file contains just a list of partition names.

The /etc/fstab file is used for other purposes in BSD. The **mount** program reads this file if the **-a** option is used and mounts all the partitions in it. The **fsck** program reads this file if no file system is specified and checks all the file systems listed.

fsck is normally run as part of the boot script in UNIX. It automatically corrects any errors in the file system. If errors are found, it is rerun to recheck for any further discrepancies.

Writing Files to Disk

MS-DOS has a BUFFERS statement in the CONFIG.SYS that determines how many memory buffers will be used for reading and writing to disk. All these buffers are written out to disk by the time a program ends and you return to the prompt. You can turn power off at the prompt without losing any data.

The UNIX system uses a large number of disk buffers, usually sized to be about 10 percent of the total memory. When a program ends, the contents of the disk buffers are not automatically written to disk. Every 30 seconds or so, a function called **sync** is started that writes all the memory buffers to disk. If you power-off the computer, you will probably lose data—the buffers that have not been written. You should turn off the computer only after you have shut the system down according to the instructions given later in this chapter.

Backing Up Files

The MS-DOS BACKUP and RESTORE programs provide for backing up the hard disk to floppies and for restoring any or all of the files from floppies. The corresponding programs for UNIX are **dump** and **restor**. The latter may also be named **restore**. The storage medium for the dump is usually a tape drive. The dump can back up any or all files on a single file system.

The MS-DOS BACKUP program permits you to back up all files or files that have not been backed up since a particular date or which have changed since the last backup. The UNIX **dump** program works with the criteria of both a date and a level. The /etc/dumpdate file keeps track of the dates associated with the last dump at each level. Level 0 specifies all the files. Level 1 specifies all files that have changed since the last level-0 dump. Level 2 specifies all files that have changed since the last level-1 dump.

You normally schedule a level-0 (all files) dump on an infrequent basis, say once a year. Then the level-1 dumps would be scheduled monthly; the level-2 dumps weekly, and the level-3 dumps daily. Note that you do not specify the filenames for **dump**. All files that match the level criteria are copied. The dump command syntax is

```
dump -level file-system
```

You can specify an alternative dump device with **-f** *dump-device*. For example,

```
dump -2f /dev/tp0   /usr
```

performs a level-2 dump of the file system mounted on **/usr** to a device named **tp0**.

Like RESTORE, the UNIX **restor** command restores files to a file system. Its syntax is

```
restor options file-system file(s)
```

The **restor** command has options to list the table of contents on the dump tape (**-t**), restore all files from the tape (**-r**), restore (extract) only particular files (**-x**), and restore interactively (**-i**). For example,

```
restor -tf /dev/tp0
```

lists the table of contents of the dump tape on **/dev/tp0**.

Some versions of UNIX do not have **dump** and **restor**. You will need to use the backup programs listed in Chapter 16.

Workout Backup

---

1. Log on as root.
2. Tell other users to log off.

```
$ wall
System going down
in 5 minutes - log off
<control-D>
```

3. When users have logged off, execute shutdown to single-user mode and sync.

```
$ shutdown now
$ sync
```

4. Perform a dump onto the default device you use. Use **df** to give the names of the file systems.

```
$ dump -3u filesystem
```

5. After the dump is done, halt the system.

```
$ halt
```

6. Power off or go back to multiuser mode after rebooting.

```
<control-D> (BSD)
init 2 (System V)
```

PROCESSES

There are many processes associated with a running UNIX system. Some are user processes and others provide system services. There is at least one process associated with each terminal that handles log-ins and which becomes the shell process for the user. There are many others that are not associated with the terminal or the user.

Daemons

daemon processes are not associated with a particular terminal. These processes execute periodically or on demand. The daemons include one that schedules other processes, one that handles mail, and ones that handle network traffic. These processes are usually started up by the boot script. To get a listing of all these processes, you can use the **-ax** option with **ps**.

Killing Processes

As superuser, you have the ability to kill any processes. Individual users have the right to kill only those processes they have created. To kill a process, you need to know the process id, which is listed on the output of the **ps** command. The kill command is

```
$ kill process-id
```

Occasionally, you may need to send other signals to a process to get it to stop. You can send the equivalent of the keyboard **intr** and **quit** keys with

```
$ kill -INTR process-id
$ kill -QUIT process-id
```

If these do not stop the process, you can enter

```
$ kill -9 process-id
```

or

```
$ kill -KILL process-id
```

The **-9** or **-KILL** options send a "kill" signal to the process, which cannot be ignored.

Executing Commands at Particular Times

One of the daemon processes (**cron**) runs other processes periodically. The **/etc/crontab** file lists the processes with an indication of the period. The syntax for each line in this table is

```
hour minute month day day-of-week command-string
```

The *command-string* is run when the time matches that given by the period specified by *hour*, *minute*, *month*, *day*, and *day-of-week*. Each of these values can be multiple values (such as **1, 2, 3**) or can be ***** for don't care. The values for *day-of-week* begin with 0 for Sunday.

THE BOOT PROCEDURE

The booting procedure for MS-DOS starts with a program on ROM in the hardware reading the boot sector of a disk. The small program loaded from that sector then loads the MS-DOS program—the hidden MSDOS.SYS file. That program reads the CONFIG.SYS file for further information as how to configure itself, including table sizes (e.g., FILES = 20), and device drivers

(DEVICE=ANSI.SYS). Once configuration is complete, it executes the AUTOEXEC.BAT.

The UNIX booting procedure follows a similar pattern. However, configuration parameters are set when the system is determined. The hardware boot program reads a boot program off the disk. This boot program then loads the /vmunix (sometimes named /unix) program from the root directory of the root file system. The operating system contains all the device drivers. Each device driver is run to test for the presence of the particular device in the current hardware system. If the device is not present or not working, that information is kept in case an attempt is made to access it. To add additional drivers, you need to rebuild the system. That process is beyond the scope of this book, but descriptions are available in your system documentation.

Three processes are started up. These include two for memory management[pagedaemon (process id 2)] and process swapping [swapper (process id 0)]. A third process controls the initialization of the remainder of UNIX [init (process id 1)].

The system can start up in single-user mode, which has only the console terminal. In single-user mode, only the root file system is mounted. The system is fairly bare—no daemons are running. To get to multiuser mode, you either exit with a <control-D> for single user (BSD) or type init 2 (System V). Some systems can be set up to go into multiuser mode automatically .

In BSD, the /etc/rc script is run (similar to AUTOEXEC.BAT). This script invokes the /etc/rc.local script. Rather than changing /etc/rc, all local boot modifications are usually contained in /etc/rc.local. The init process then looks in the /etc/ttys file and executes a program (usually getty) for each terminal listed in it. The getty program outputs a "login:" prompt on the terminal.

Under System V, the /etc/inittab file contains information as to what programs to execute when init is run. These programs perform operations similar to those contained in the /etc/rc and /etc/ttys files.

When a user responds to a "login:" prompt, getty starts the login program. That program requests a password and validates it against the one contained in the /etc/passwd file. If the password is valid, login sets up the environment and prints the message of the day (/etc/motd). Finally, it executes the program specified for the user in /etc/passwd, usually a shell. The shell executes its startup script (e.g., .profile) and then prompts the user for input. When a user exits the shell (with a <control-D>), init is notified and it restarts the getty program for that terminal.

SHUTDOWN

With MS-DOS, you can turn power off when you are at the command prompt, and thus no program is running. At this point all disk buffers have been written to files, and the hard disk is up to date. With UNIX, the system must be shut down systematically. Many users can be running programs. If the disk buffers are not written out, data can be lost.

The **shutdown** command stops multiuser mode gracefully. The syntax is

shutdown *time message*

The *time* can be specified relative to current time or as absolute time. The optional *message* will be broadcast to all users. Users are warned periodically of the impending shutdown.

Once in single-user mode, the **halt** command kills the daemon processes and executes **sync**, which writes the operating system disk buffers to the hard disk. After this command completes, you can turn the power off. You can include an **-h** option on the **shutdown** command to execute halt automatically.

Workout Shutdown

---

1. When other users are not on your system, try shutting down the system following the instructions given. Then restart the system.
2. If you are on a single-user system, wait 60 seconds without typing a command, then shut down the system, but do not run **halt**. Turn power off and back on. Then restart the system and note what **fsck** does to recover files.

DEVICES

Under MS-DOS, there are certain special names, such as CON, that may be used in place of filenames. These cause a command to input or output to or from that device. For example, COPY CON TEMP causes the input from the keyboard to go to a file called TEMP.

In UNIX, all devices have filenames that can be used in place of a regular filename. Associated with every device is at least one special file in the /dev directory, such as **/dev/tty01** and **/dev/lp**. The names vary depending on the system. An ordinary user can use the name of a device as a filename in commands, such as

```
cat one.doc > /dev/tty01
```

Many devices are readable and writable only by the superuser, as writing directly to the disk can destroy the file system.

Each special filename represents a device driver for a particular piece of hardware. A device driver is similar to that referred to in DEVICE=XXX statements in the MS-DOS CONFIG.SYS. Each file has two numbers associated with it. The major device number represents a particular type of hardware, and the minor device number represents a particular piece of hardware. These numbers are listed in the output of **ls -l**.

There are two different kind of drivers: character and block. The character driver reads and writes individual characters; the block driver reads and writes a disk block. Disk partitions have two drivers, one of each type. A disk character driver has the same name as the block driver, with an "**r**" appended at the end. The **fsck** program uses the character driver to repair the file system.

There are two special device names that are useful in writing shell scripts: the **/dev/tty** device represents the log-in terminal of a user; the **/dev/null** is the universal data dump—nothing is written to it.

OTHER TYPES OF FILES

Some systems have two other types of files. The first is the socket (**s**), which is used for communication between two processes. The second is the pipe (**p**), which acts as a persistent pipeline. One process can write to it and another process can read from it. The two processes do not have to be run with the | operator in the same command.

NETWORKS

The setup and administration of networks is beyond the scope of this book. Most of the setup is performed when you follow the vendor instructions for installing the system. Networks can include the Network File System (NFS) and the Distributed File System (DFS) for remote sharing of files and "Yellow Pages" or BIND/Hesiod for keeping directories of users and hosts consistent on a network. For a system that is on a network, there is one additional file of which you should be aware . The names and Internet addresses of other host systems are kept in a file called **/etc/hosts**. Each line of this file contains

```
Internet-address hostname(s)
```

The *Internet-address* is four numbers separated by periods. The *hostname(s)* are the names by which the host at that address is known: for example,

```
27.32.12.10   dukemvs.ac.duke.edu
```

A portion of the Internet address for an organization is assigned by Stanford Research Institute's Network Information Center. The same organization assigns organizational names, which are used as part of the host name. Your organization may already have a number and name assigned to it. Even though you may not be connected to the Internet initially, you may want to obtain a number and name for either your local organization or Stanford. This will avoid having to change it later, if you do connect.

SYSTEM STATUS

There are several programs that provide information on the status of the system. The names may vary from system to system. The state of the printer queue can be determined with **lpq**. Memory usage can be seen with **vmstat**. The status of the network is shown by **netstat**.

Workout Administration

1. Check out the devices on your system.

```
$ ls -l /dev | more
```

   See if you can identify which devices are associated with which pieces of hardware.
2. Try **lpq**, **vmstat**, and **netstat** to see what the output looks like.

FOR FURTHER INFORMATION

AT&T. 1988. *UNIX System V/386 Administrator's Guide.* Englewood Cliffs, N.J.: Prentice Hall. System V specific administrative narrative.

AT&T. 1988. *UNIX System V/386 Administrator's Reference.* Englewood Cliffs, N.J.: Prentice Hall. Manual for programs for administrators.

AT&T. 1988. *UNIX System V Administrator's Guide.* Englewood Cliffs, N.J.: Prentice Hall. System V specific administrative narrative.

Fiedler, David, Bruce Hunter, and Ben Smith. 1991. *UNIX System V Release 4 Administration.*Hayden.

Frisch, Aeleen. 1991. *Essential System Administration.*O'Reilly.

Nemeth, Evi, Snyder, Garth, and Seebass, Scott. 1989. *UNIX System Administration Handbook.* Englewood Cliffs, N.J.: Prentice Hall. This is an excellent guide for system administrators.

Thomas, Rebecca, and Farrow, Rik. 1989. *UNIX Administration Guide for System V.* Englewood Cliffs, N.J.: Prentice Hall.

COMMAND SUMMARY

Become superuser	**su**
Writing to users	**wall**
Make file system	**mkfs**
Mount file system	**mount** *partition-device directory*
Unmount file system	**umount** *partition-device*
Disk usage	
File system	**df**
Directory	**du**
File checking	**fsck**
Writing buffers to disk	**sync**
Backing up files	**dump** *-level file-system*
Dump device	**-f** *dump-device*
Restoring files	**restor** or **restore**
Table of contents	**-t**
Restore all files	**-r**
Restore particular files	**-x**
Interactive	**-i**
Killing processes	**kill** *process-id*
	kill *-signal process-id*
Shutdown	**shutdown** *time message*
and halt	**-h**
Halt system	**halt**

Administrative files
    Terminal ports   `/etc/ttys` (`etc/inittab`—System V)
    Message of the day   `/etc/motd`
    Users and passwords   `/etc/passwd`
    Groups   `/etc/groups`
    Messages   `/etc/msgs` (BSD) or `/usr/news` (System V)
    Scheduled events   `/etc/crontab`
    Disk partition values   `/etc/disktab`
    Lost files   `/lost+found`
    File system table   `/etc/fstab` (BSD)
    Checking table for **fsck**   `/etc/fstab` (BSD) or
                                   `/etc/checklist` (System V)

    Startup files   `/etc/rc` and `/etc/rc.local` (BSD)
                                   `/etc/inittab` (System V)
    Host names and addresses   `/etc/hosts`

13 | TEXT PROCESSING

Paginate, paginate, paginate

Word-processing programs in MS-DOS provide the ability to create formatted output. The standard editors in UNIX are line-oriented editors. Separate text formatting programs such as **nroff** and **troff** turn commands intermixed with text into formatted output. Unlike common MS-DOS word processors, the format is definitely *not* "What You See Is What You Get."

PROGRAMS

Two text processing programs output text files as formatted text for either monospaced printers (**nroff**) or typesetting printers (such as Postscript printers) (**troff**). These programs are run as either

```
nroff  file-name
troff  file-name
```

These programs will be referred to generically as **nroff**, as the command sets are basically the same.[1]

---

[1] With **troff**, there are additional commands embedded in the text, in particular the font commands, which begin with a backslash \.

Commands in these programs are lines that begin with a period or an apostrophe. The former is familiar to MS-DOS users of Wordstar. Command lines may include some parameters. All other lines not starting with a period or apostrophe are treated as text to be formatted.

As an extension of these programs, there are preprocessing programs, which can operate on mathematical expressions (**eqn**), tables (**tbl**), and pictures (**pic**). You describe an item using the structure as described by the respective program. The output from the program are files containing **nroff** commands and text. These files are run through **nroff** to obtain the final printed output.[2]

Macro Package

The basic commands in **nroff** are fairly primitive. The commands can be combined into macros. To simplify and standardize their use, a number of macro packages are available. The most common are **ms** for manuscripts, **mm** for memorandums, and **man** for manual pages. These should be distributed with your **nroff** or **troff** programs. If not, check with your system administrator.

The macro packages include formatting for paragraphs, headers, and footers. They are specified with an option on the command line:

    -mname-of-macro-package

such as

    nroff -ms my-file

The corresponding macro package is in a file named by **/usr/lib/tmac.**name-of-macro-package, such as **/usr/lib/tmac.s** for the **-ms** package. To be differentiated from primitive **nroff** commands, macro commands usually use uppercase letters, although this is not universal.

FORMATTING

Most macro packages contain a standard set of commands for formatting paragraphs and pages. We'll examine some of the basic commands, starting with some of the macro commands for the **ms** package and ending with

---

[2] There is a postprocessing program called **col** that is used to remove reverse line motions from the output of **nroff** for devices that cannot support them.

some primitive commands. The **mm** package has more elaborate commands than **ms**, but it may not be available on your system.

Paragraphs

With MS-DOS word processors, everything you type until you hit an enter key is placed in a paragraph. With **nroff -ms**, everything up to a paragraph format (`.PP`) command is output as a paragraph. The new-lines at the end of each line in the text are ignored. By default, the lines are filled up to the size of the output line and justified. Changing the fill mode and justification will be described shortly. The `.PP` command inserts a blank line into the text and indents the first line by the paragraph indent size (which is defaulted to a half-inch). A blank line (one without any characters) can also be treated as a paragraph format line. An example of input is:

```
.PP
This is the first paragraph, which continues
on as many lines as necessary.
.PP
This is the second paragraph, which also continues
along
with as many words as required.
```

Assuming that the margins were narrow, the corresponding output would look as follows:

> This is the first paragraph, which contin-
> ues on as many lines as necessary.
> This is the second paragraph, which
> also continues along with as many words as
> required.

Paragraphs can be indented using the `.IP` command. Optionally, a string can be placed in the margin by giving a *tag* after the command. For example,

```
.IP "(1)"
This is an indented paragraph continued onto here.
```

will appear as

> (1) This is an indented paragraph
>   continued onto here.

Headings

You can add subheadings to your text using the `.SH` command. Everything up to the next `.PP` command is treated as a heading and is output flush left in boldface type. For example,

```
.SH
Section One
.PP
Paragraph one
.SH
Section Two
.PP
Paragraph two
```

turns into

Section One
    Paragraph one
Section Two
    Paragraph two

Headings can be numbered using the `.NH` command. Optionally, you can specify the level of the number. The command keeps track of the values used for each level. For example,

```
.NH
Section One
.PP
Paragraph one
.NH
Section Two
.PP
Paragraph two
```

turns into

1. Section One
    Paragraph one
2. Section Two
    Paragraph two

Headers and Footers

Page headers and footers are specified by setting their values with the define string command (`.ds`). The six possible locations of these are:

Left top header	`LT`
Right top header	`RT`
Center top header	`CT`
Left footer	`LF`
Right footer	`RF`
Center footer	`CF`

The left and right headers and footers are placed relative to the left and right margins. The center header and footer are centered in the line. The default footer is the current page number centered at the bottom. The page headers (`LT`, `RT`, and `CT`) may be specified with a different command on your **nroff**. To specify the centered footer on a page, you could use

```
.ds CF Footer
```

Fonts

The font commands set the output font for all the following text until the setting is changed. Three standard fonts are:

roman(plain)	`.R`
boldface	`.B`
italics	`.I`

If you only want to change the font for a single set of words, you can specify them after the command, as

boldface	`.B` *words*
italics	`.I` *words*

For example,

```
.R
This is plain
.I
but this is italic
.B
and this is bold.
.R
```

```
This is again plain and just
.I this
is italic and just
.B this
is bold.
```

creates

```
This is plain but this is italic and this is
bold. This is again plain and just this is
italic and just this is bold.
```

Footnotes

You can create footnotes, which are printed at the bottom of the page. You need to include any identifying marks, such as an asterisk. The footnote begins with `.FS` and ends with `.FE`. For example,

```
There will be a footnote placed (*)
.FS
* This is the footnote
.FE
in the text here.
...
```

creates a footnote on the current page as

```
There will be a footnote placed (*) in the
text here.
...
_ _ _ _ _ _ _ _ _ _ _ _ _ _ _ _ _ _ _ _ _ _ _ _ _ _
* This is the footnote
```

Turning Off Formatting

You can keep lines exactly as they appear in the text by using the display commands (`.DS` and `.DE`). No formatting is performed on lines between these two commands. If you do not specify an option after `.DS`, the lines will be indented. To move them to the left margin, use `.DS L`.

Character Interpretation

You may wish to have a line beginning with a period interpreted as text rather than as a command. To do this you preface the line with `\&`. For example,

```
\&.PP
```

will cause ".PP" to be interpreted as text to be formatted.

You can create unpaddable blanks by using "\ ". If a line is justified with both margins, additional spaces may be added between words. An unpaddable blank between words prevents additional spaces from being inserted at that position. Multiple words separated by unpaddable blanks are treated as a single argument, just as strings with quotes around them. For example,

```
.B something\ to\ blank
```

works the same as

```
.B "something to blank"
```

To get a backslash to print, you use the escape sequence \e.

Primitive Commands

Even though the macro packages provide most of your needs, you may run into situations where you need to use the primitive commands. The begin a new page (.bp) command terminates the current page and starts a new one. The line length (.11)command sets the length of the output line. The page offset command (.po) sets the offset of the left margin in the output. You can skip one or more lines with the .sp command. You can optionally specify the number of lines to skip: for example,

Skip one line	`.sp`
Skip three lines	`.sp 3`

The break command (.br) causes the previous line to end without justification. The next text line will be output on a new line. You can center the next line with the .ce command. Comments—lines that will not be interpreted or output—can be included in a file by prefacing them with \".

You can set tab stops using the .ta command and specifying the values for each subsequent tab stop. The tab character can be specified with the .tc command. For example,

```
.ta 5 10 15 20
<tab>1<tab>2<tab>3
```

produces

```
1     2     3
```

You can set temporary indentation of the next line with the `.ti` command. You specify the number of spaces after the command as

```
.ti 10
```

As shown with headers and footers, you can define strings with the `.ds` command. The format is

```
.ds name "string"
```

The *name* can be one or two characters long. When using value of *name*, you specify it with `\*`*name* if the name is one character long or with `\*(`*name* if it is two characters long. For example,

```
.ds ME Kenneth
I am \*(ME.
```

produces

```
I am Kenneth.
```

Filling and Justifying

If fill mode is on, each output line is filled up with words to the maximum length. If fill mode is off, each output line contains the words that appear on a line of input. The no fill command (`.nf`) turns fill off and the fill command (`.fi`) turns it back on.

Justification is the act of adding extra spaces to the output text to make it line up with either the left or right margins or both, or to center it. Justification (also called adjusting) can be turned off by `.na` and turned on with `.ad`.

Words can be kept intact or can be hyphenated automatically to break them between lines. Hyphenation can be turned off with `.nh` and on with `.hy`.

Defining Your Own Macros

In addition to using the macro packages, you can define your own macros. Start a macro definition with `.de` *name* and end it with a single line of `...` The values of the arguments passed to a macro can be used inside it with `\\$1`, `\\$2`, `\\$3`, and so on: for example,

```
.de MY
.sp 2
.ce
\\$1
.sp 2
..
```

Using this macro as

```
.MY "This is a test"
```

produces the sequence

```
.sp 2
.ce
This is a test
.sp 2
```

Workout nroff

1. Take a short formatted page of a book and try writing the corresponding **nroff** file that could produce it. Or try creating the following file, say **nroff.test**

```
.sp 3
.NH
First part
.PP
This is a simple test of the
.B nroff
to see how the system works (*).
.FS
* This is
.I
not
.R
a full demonstration.
.FE
.PP
This is the second paragraph of the first part
.NH
Second part
```

```
.PP
This is the first paragraph of the second part.
.IP (1)
A list is usually indented. But it doesn't have to
be.
These lines will be indented
.DS L
These lines will appear
just as you see them (without wrapping).
.DE
.PP
This is the last paragraph.
```

2. Run the file through **nroff** as:

```
$ nroff -ms nroff.test > nroff.out
```

Then examine the output using **more**, with

```
$ more nroff.out
```

If you have a printer available, you can redirect the output of **nroff** to either **lp** or **lpr**.

TEXT PROCESSING UNDER UNIX

If you have access to a word processor under UNIX, such as WordPerfect, you may find that using **nroff** to do formatting is a bit complex. Most WordPerfect commands mirror **nroff** commands. Unlike WordPerfect, the formatted output of **nroff** is not immediately available. An advantage of using **nroff** is that text files containing **nroff** commands are interchangeable among all UNIX operating systems that support the program. They are searchable and processible by UNIX text programs, such as **grep** and **awk**. Because they contain embedded control characters, WordPerfect files are less amenable to use with other UNIX programs.

FOR FURTHER INFORMATION

Look at the **man** pages for **ms**. Read the **nroff** documentation that accompanied your system. Ask your system administrator about macro packages available on your system.

Brown, Constance C., Falk, Jack L., and Sperline, Richard D. 1986. *Preparing Documents with UNIX*. Englewood Cliffs, N.J.: Prentice Hall.

Dougherty, Dale, and O'Reilly, Tim. 1989. *UNIX Text Processing*. Sebastopol, Calif.: O'Reilly and Associates.

Emerson, Sandra L., and Paulsell, Karen. 1987. *Troff Typesetting for UNIX Systems*.

Kernighan, B. W. 1984. *A Troff Tutorial*. UNIX Documentation Set.

Lesk, M. E. 1984. *Tbl—A Program to Format Tables*. UNIX Documentation Set.

McGilton, Henry, and McNabb, Mary. 1991. *Typesetting Tables on the UNIX System*. Sebastopol, Calif.: O'Reilly and Associates.

COMMAND SUMMARY

Text formatting
    Fixed size   `nroff -m`*macro-name file-name*
    Typeset   `troff -m`*macro-name file-name*

ms macro package
    Paragraphs   `.PP`
    Indented paragraph   `.IP` *tag*
    Subheadings   `.SH`
    Numbered headings   `.NH`
    Headers and footers   `.ds` *where string*
        Left top header   `LT`
        Right top header   `RT`
        Center top header   `CT`
        Left footer   `LF`
        Right footer   `RF`
        Center footer   `CF`
    Fonts
        Roman(plain)   `.R`
        Boldface   `.B`
        Italics   `.I`
        Boldface   `.B` *words*
        Italics   `.I` *words*
    Footnotes
        Start   `.FS`
        End   `.FE`
    Turning off formatting
        Display start   `.DS`
        Display start
           (at left margin)   `.DS L`

Display end	`.DE`
Character interpretation	
Start of line	`\&`
Unpaddable blank	`\<space>`
Backslash	`\e`
Primitive commands	
Begin a new page	`.bp`
Line length	`.ll`
Page offset	`.po`
Skip one line	`.sp`
Skip *number* lines	`.sp` *number*
Break	`.br`
Center next line	`.ce`
Comments	`\"`
Tab stops	`.ta` *values(s)*
Tab characters	`.tc` *character*
Indentation	`.ti` *value*
Define strings	`.ds` *name* "*string*"
String replacement	`\\*`*name* or `\(*`*name*
Filling and justifying	
Fill off	`.nf`
Fill on	`.fi`
Justification off	`.na`
Justification on	`.ad`
Hyphenation	
Off	`.nh`
On	`.hy`
Macro definitions	`.de` *name*
End	`..`
Arguments	`\\$`*number*

14 | TEXT REVISION SYSTEMS

What changed?

The maintenance and revision of text files can occupy a large percentage of a user's time. UNIX has a number of tools for helping keep track of changes. These are typically used for program source control, but they can be applied to manuals, procedures, and other documents. One common system is the Source Code Control System, described here.

FILE DIFFERENCE PROGRAM

You may just need to compare the differences between two text files. The **diff** program provides that capability. It works like the MS-DOS FC program. It outputs the line-by-line differences between files, including the lines that have been added, deleted, or changed. The program incorporates some intelligence in determining what alterations have been made. The syntax is

diff *first-file second-file*

It outputs a list of operations, as additions (**a**), deletions (**d**), and changes (**c**) in the form

first-file-line-numbers operation second-file-line-numbers

The *first-file-line-numbers* and *second-file-line-numbers* may be either single numbers or a range of numbers separated by commas. The lines that will be deleted or changed from the first file are listed after each operation with

```
< line-from-first-file
```

The lines to be added or changed into the second file are listed with

```
> line-from-second-file
```

For example, suppose that you had two files, **version-1** and **version-2**. **version-1** contained

```
line 1
line 2
line 4
```

and **version-2** contained

```
line 1
line 3
line 4
```

If you ran

```
diff version-1 version-2
```

the output would be

```
2c2
< line 2
---
> line 3
```

This means that if line 2 in **version-1** were changed from "**line 2**" to "**line 3**", it would match **version-2**.

You can run **diff** with the **-e** option to create a set of **ed** commands that can transform **first-file** into **second-file**. In this example,

```
diff -e version-1 version-2
```

would produce the output

```
2c
line 3
.
```

The output of **diff** is similar to what is stored by source control systems. Instead of saving every copy of every version, they save one copy of a file, along with the commands necessary to transform it into other versions.

Workout diff

1. See the differences between **one.doc** and **two.doc**

   $ **diff one.doc two.doc**

2. See the edit commands with:

   $ **diff -e one.doc two.doc**

SOURCE CODE CONTROL SYSTEM

Most MS-DOS word processing programs keep a backup copy of your files. However, you usually cannot retrieve a version that is three or four prior to your current one. The Source Code Control System (SCCS) permits you to keep track of numerous revisions and to go back to any previous version. There are other available systems, such as the Revision Control System (RCS), which permit the same types of operations as those in SCCS.

SCCS keeps track of changes to text in your file with its own control file. Each set of changes is called a delta. Every time a delta is applied to text, a new version is created. Each version is identified with a SCCS IDentification string (SID), which is a numeric value consisting of *release-number.level-number*.[1] The original text has a SID of 1.1.

---

[1] The SID can be expanded to include branches. These are changes that are not applied to all versions. The syntax for branch numbering is

release-number.level-number.branch-number.sequence-number

SCCS has many programs associated with it, such as **admin** and **delta**. These are run as standard UNIX commands. Some versions of SCCS permit you to specify these as arguments on the command line to a **sccs** program, such as

sccs admin *admin-arguments*

You should check with your system administrator to see which version you are using.

Creating a Control File

The first step is to create an SCCS control file with the **admin** program. The syntax is

admin -i*original-file control-file*

The *original-file* contains the original text. The name specified for *control-file* is usually **s.***original-file*. The *control-file* is in SCCS format and should not be altered by you directly. The control file will contain Version 1.1. You may get a warning message "No id keywords" when you first **admin** a file. The meaning of that message will be examined shortly under ID Keywords.

There are many options for **admin**, for allowing multiple simultaneous edits, specifying which users can make changes, and so forth. Most of the values for these options can be changed after the file is created.

Retrieving a Version

You retrieve the latest version of a file using the **get** command. You can get a file for read-only purposes or for editing. To get a read-only version, enter

get *control-file*

You can get a previous version by using the **-r***sid-number* option on **get**. To get an editable version, enter

get -e *control-file*

When you get a file for editing, a new file called a "p-file" is created. The p-file is used by SCCS in determining the changes in the new version. The next version number is output when you retrieve a file for editing.

When you get a file, SCCS starts with the original version and applies all the successive changes to it. If you want to change to a new release number rather than just a new level number, you specify that when getting the file for editing with the **-r**`new-release-number` option.

If you get a file for editing by mistake, you can run **unget** to cancel the update. You need to cancel since SCCS will have noted in the control file and the p-file that a potential update was outstanding. The syntax is

```
unget control-file
```

Recording Changes

Once you have finished making changes to the text, you place them into the `control-file` with **delta**. The syntax is

```
delta control-file
```

The program will request comments that you enter to describe why the changes were made. **delta** reads the p-file that was created when the text was retrieved to determine the differences. Only the differences (similar to the output of **diff**) are stored in the control file.

Workout SCCS

1. Place the **presidents** file under SCCS control, and erase the original file.

```
$ admin -ipresidents s.presidents
$ rm presidents
```

2. Retrieve the latest version of the file.

```
$ get s.presidents
1.1
42 lines
```

3. Erase the read-only version and get an editable version.

```
$ rm presidents
```

You may get a prompt such as

```
rm: override protection 444 for presidents ?
```

Answer with **y**

```
$ get -e s.presidents
1.1
new delta 1.2
42 lines
```

4. Edit **presidents** with either **vi** or **emacs**. Add the following line at the end:

   42 Clinton William Jefferson

5. Store away the changes you made in the file with **delta**. Enter

```
$ delta s.presidents
comments?
        New president January 20, 1993.
<control-D>
1 inserted
0 deleted
41 unchanged
```

ID Keywords

A SCCS file can include ID keywords which are replaced with values such as the SID or the time of a delta. The replacements occur when a file is retrieved in read-only mode. When a file is gotten for editing, these keywords are not replaced. A keyword id has the form %*id*%. Table 14–1 lists some of the ids.[2] You can include keyword ids in your text to document the revision level. For example, with **nroff -ms**, you might include:

```
.ds CF "Printed %H% %T% from %M%"
.ds LT "Revision %R%.%L% created %G% %U%"
```

---

[2] Some versions may not have all these keyword IDs.

TABLE 14–1 Keyword IDs

Module name (name of file)	%M%
Current date (YY/MM/DD)	%D%
Current date (MM/DD/YY)	%H%
Current time (HH:MM:SS)	%T%
Date new delta created (YY/MM/DD)	%E%
Date new delta created (MM/DD/YY)	%G%
Time new delta created (HH:MM:SS)	%U%
String recognizable by **what** program "@(#)"	%Z%
Release	%R%
Level	%L%
SID identification (%R%.%L%.%B%.%S%)	%I%
String for **what** program plus SID (%Z%%M%<tab>%I%)	%W%

This would print a centered footer containing print information and a left header containing revision information.

If you do not have any id keywords in your file, you may get a warning such as "No id keywords" when you check the file in.

The **what** Command

There are some keyword ids, such as **%Z%**, which cause the substitution of "@(#)" in a file. This special string is included in many executable program files.[3] The **what** program searches files for this string and prints out the characters that follow until a terminating character occurs. To see what the version of a program is, type

    what *name-of-program*

For example,

    what /bin/csh

---

[3] C programmers can include it in their programs with declarations such as

    static char * version = "%W%";

will print out the source file names, the revisions, and the dates of all the parts of **/bin/csh**. If you were having trouble with a particular program, this information would be useful to your system administrator or other person who is trying to determine the problem.

You may see multiple lines output, as each program is made up of many files.

Auxiliary Programs

There are several auxiliary programs in SCCS. The remove delta program (**rmdel**) removes the delta that created the last version. To remove multiple deltas, you need to execute it multiple times. The syntax is

```
rmdel -rrelease.level control-file
```

You output the differences between two versions using **sccsdiff**. The syntax is

```
sccsdiff -rrelease-1.level-1 -rrelease-2.level-2 control-file
```

This will print the differences between *release-1.level-1* and *release-2.level-2*.

Comments on a version can be changed with **cdc**. The syntax is

```
cdc -rrelease.level control-file
```

You print the history of the revisions with **prs**. Its syntax is

```
prs control-file
```


REVISION CONTROL SYSTEM

The RCS (Revision Control System) is a revision system that works in much the same way as SCCS. It appends a "**,v**" to the file names in creating a control file and uses **RCS** as the directory for these files. The check-in program (**ci**) is used to create and check in source files.

```
ci presidents
```

creates **RCS/presidents,v** if it does not already exist. You check out a read-only version of a file with **co**, as

```
co presidents
```

To check out the file for editing (with a lock on the file), you use the `-l` option, as

```
co -l presidents
```

Check the file back in and record with changes with `ci`:

```
ci presidents
```

The revision listing program is `rlog` and the difference program is `rcsdiff`.

Keeping Generated Files Up to Date

Each revision control file keeps track of the changes to one source file. You may have a final output file that is a combination of files. To form a version of the final output, you can get the latest revision of each individual file and put them together. However, it takes processing time to perform the retrieval operations. The **make** program can eliminate unnecessary operations.

Let's take a simple example. Suppose that you have files which contain chapters, which will be combined into sections. To make up the total book, you might run the following commands as a script file called **make-book.**

```
cat chapter-1.doc chapter-2.doc chapter-3.doc > section-1.doc
cat chapter-4.doc chapter-5.doc > section-2.doc
cat chapter-6.doc chapter-7.doc > section-3.doc
cat section-1.doc section-2.doc section-3.doc > book
```

Every time you run this script, every command will be executed. To save processing time, you only need to execute the commands for those files that have changed. For example, if **chapter-1** changed, you only need to execute

```
cat chapter-1.doc chapter-2.doc chapter-3.doc > section-1.doc
cat section-1.doc section-2.doc section-3.doc > book
```

The **make** program helps eliminate the extra commands. To use **make**, you need to create a **Makefile**, which gives a list of rules. These rules are of the form

```
target : dependencies
<tab>commands
```

If the *target* file has a later modification time than all the files named as *dependencies*, **make** assumes that the *target* file is up to date. If not, it executes the *commands*. In our example we would have a **Makefile** with

```
book: section-1.doc section-2.doc section-3.doc
<tab>cat section-1.doc section-2.doc section-3.doc > book
section-1.doc:chapter-1.doc chapter-2.doc chapter-3.doc
<tab>cat chapter-1.doc chapter-2.doc chapter-3.doc > section-1.doc
section-2.doc:chapter-4.doc chapter-5.doc
<tab>cat chapter-4.doc chapter-5.doc > section-2.doc
section-3.doc:chapter-6.doc chapter-7.doc
<tab>cat chapter-6.doc chapter-7.doc > section-3.doc
```

Suppose that **chapter-1.doc** changed. When you run **make**, it reads the **Makefile** and determines that **section-1.doc** is dependent on **chapter-1.doc** and that **chapter-1.doc** has a later modification time than **section-1.doc**. It then runs the command

```
cat chapter-1.doc chapter-2.doc chapter-3.doc > section-1.doc
```

It also notes that **book** is dependent on **section-1.doc** and therefore it will also run

```
cat section-1.doc section-2.doc section-3.doc > book
```

You could have added rules for retrieving files from SCCS. For example, to retrieve **chapter-1.doc**, you could have

```
chapter-1.doc : s.chapter-1.doc
<tab>get s.chapter-1.doc
```

The **make** program has many options. You can specify a particular target by giving the name, as

```
make target
```

For example,

```
make section-1.doc
```

would cause only

```
<tab>cat chapter-1.doc chapter-2.doc chapter-3.doc > section-1.doc
```

to be executed. If you do not specify a target, it will use the target of the
first rule as the file to check.

Normally, **make** looks in the current directory for a rule file called
Makefile or **makefile**, but you can specify the file using **-f**
makefile-name. For example, if the rules were kept in **book.mak**, you
would use

```
make -f book.mak
```

You do not have to specify any dependencies. If you do not, **make**
performs the commands unconditionally. For example, if the file contained

```
clean :
<tab>rm *.bak
```

then

```
make clean
```

would cause

```
rm *bak
```

to be executed.

You can use macros within your **Makefile**. A macro is defined with

name=text

and used in the **Makefile** with

$(*name*)

The example above could have been specified with macros as:

```
CHAPTERS = chapter-1.doc chapter-2.doc chapter-3.doc
SECTIONS = section-1.doc section-2.doc section-3.doc
SECTION-1 = chapter-1.doc chapter-2.doc chapter-3.doc
SECTION-2 = chapter-4.doc chapter-5.doc
SECTION-3 = chapter-6.doc chapter-7.doc
```

```
book: $(SECTIONS)
<tab>cat $(SECTIONS) > book
section-1.doc:$(SECTION-1)
<tab>cat $(SECTION-1) > section-1.doc
section-2.doc:$(SECTION-2)
<tab>cat $(SECTION-2) > section-2.doc
section-3.doc:$(SECTION-3)
<tab>cat $(SECTION-3) > section-3.doc
```

There are numerous features to **make** to cut down on the number of rules that must be listed. For example, there are many inferred rules that are based on the suffix of files. Consult the references for further information.

The **touch** program is used to bring the modification time of a file up to the current time. If you **touch** a target, it will have a later time than its dependencies, and the commands will not be executed.

FOR FURTHER INFORMATION

Feldman, S. I. 1978. make: *A Program for Maintaining Computer Programs.* UNIX Documentation Set.

Silverberg, Israel. 1992. *Source File Management with SCCS.* Englewood Cliffs, N.J.: Prentice Hall.

Talbott, Steve. 1989. *Managing Projects with* make. Sebastopol, Calif.: O'Reilly and Associates.

Tondo, Clovis L., Nathanson, Andrew, and Yount, Eden. 1992. *Mastering* make. Englewood Cliffs, N.J.: Prentice Hall.

COMMAND SUMMARY

File difference program	**diff** *first-file second-file*
Editing commands	**-e**
Source code control system	
Creating control file	**admin -i***original-file control-file*
Retrieving a version	**get** *control-file*
Previous version	**-r***sid-number*
Get editable version	**get -e** *control-file*
Update release	**-r***new-release-number*
Unget version	**unget** *control-file*
Recording changes	**delta** *control-file*

ID keywords
    See Table 14–1
SID   *release.level*
What version   **what** *name-of-program*
Remove delta   **rmdel -r***release.level control-file*
Differences **sccsdiff -r***release-1.level-1* **-r***release-2.level-2 control-file*
Comment changes   **cdc -r***release.level control-file*
Print revision history   **prs** *control-file*
Revision control system
    Check in a file   **ci** *filename*
    Check out a file   **co** *filename*
    Check out file for editing   **co -l** *filename*
    List revisions   **rlog**
    List differences   **rcsdiff**
Make
    Rule: *target* **:** *dependencies*
                               <tab>*commands*

    Macros
        Definition   *name=text*
        Usage   **$(***name***)**
    Make a target file   **make** *target*
        Specify rule file   **-f** *filename*
    Update modification time **touch** *filename(s)*

15 PATTERN SCANNING: AWK

It's fields, it's lines, it's a database

Textual manipulation of patterns has its own language in UNIX. The **awk**[1] program provides facilities for textual databases similar to those that programs such as dBase and Paradox have on MS-DOS. The **awk** program does not use index files, but rather quickly scans through text files. It has programming constructs, similar to the C language, for creating complex text manipulation programs. In this chapter, we assume an understanding of basic programming concepts, such as variables, operators, and expressions.

PATTERN-ACTION

An **awk** program specifies a set of patterns and a set of actions in the form

```
test-pattern {action}
```

Each record of input is checked for *test-pattern*. If the *test-pattern* is matched, the corresponding action is performed. If an action is listed without a pattern, it is performed on every input record. If a pattern is listed without an action, the matching record is output to the standard out-

---

[1] Named for its inventors: Aho, Weinberger, and Kernighan.

put. By default, a record is a line ending in a <new-line>, but this can be changed. For example, the **awk** program

```
/Adams/ {print}
```

prints every line that has **Adams** in it. This simple program logically does the same things as running **grep "Adams"**.

RUNNING awk

You can specify an **awk** program by naming a source file, or you can type the program on the command line. The former method is easier to learn, while the latter is used for short programs to avoid proliferation of many tiny program files. The syntax for **awk** is

```
awk -f program-file data-file
```

or

```
awk program data-file
```

If the previous program was in **test.awk** and you run this on **presidents**, the command would be

```
awk -f test.awk presidents
```

Alternatively, you can specify the program on the command line by putting it in quotes as

```
awk '/Adams/ {print}' presidents
```

The quotations make the program a single parameter and avoids having the shell interpret any special characters.

Records

Each input record is broken into fields by **awk**. The values of the individual fields can be tested and printed. By default, the fields are separated by blanks and tabs. The field values are specified by $number. For example, if the input record is

```
4 Adams John Quincy
```

the field values are

Field	Value
$1	4
$2	Adams
$3	John
$4	Quincy

The **$0** variable is the value of the entire record, so it has a value of

```
4 Adams John Quincy
```

If you wanted to print the values of some of the fields, you could code the action as

```
{ print "Last name " $2 " First name " $3}
```

This action for the record above produces

```
Last name Adams First name John
```

Variables

awk has variables that are built in and variables that you can create. The built-in values include the number of fields in the current record (**NF**), the number of the record (**NR**), the character used to separate records (**RS**), and the characters used to separate fields (**FS**). The values of these variables can be tested and printed. For example, to print the number of fields in the tenth record in a file, you would code

```
NR == 10 {print "Number fields is " NF}
```

The double equals sign is the symbol for equality.

You change the record separator and field separators by setting them to the desired values in an action. For example,

```
BEGIN { RS = ".", FS = ":"}
```

sets the record separator to a period and the field separator to a colon. The **BEGIN** pattern is described in the next section.

You can create your own variables by assigning a value to them in an action with the syntax *variable = value*. For example,

```
BEGIN { my-count = 1; my-string = "ABC"}
```

creates a variable called **my-count** and assigns it the value 1 and a variable called **my-string** and assigns it the value of **"ABC"**. If you use a variable before you have assigned a value to it, it will have the value of zero or the value of string with nothing in it, depending on the context.

Workout awk

1. Create an **awk** program file called **test1.awk**. The program is

```
/Adams/ {print "This is an Adams " $0}
/G/ {print "This has a G in it " $0}
$1 == 10 {print "The 10th president is " $0}
NR == 15 {print "The 15th record in the file is " $0}
```

2. Run this program against **presidents** with

```
$ awk -f test1.awk presidents
```

Examine the output and the program to determine which line was generated by which test-pattern/action pair.

3. Run the following in-line **awk** program:

```
$ awk '{print NR ": " $0}' presidents
```

This outputs **presidents** with each line preceded with the line number.

4. Create a program to print Cleveland's record, say **cleveland.awk**.

```
/Cleveland/ { print $3, $2, " Order ", $1}
```

5. Run this program against **presidents**.

```
$ awk -f cleveland.awk presidents
```

6. Create a program to print all presidents from the tenth to the twentieth, say **10-20.awk**.

```
$1 >= 10 && $1 <= 20 { print $3, $2, " Order ", $1}
```

7. Run the program with

```
$ awk -f 10-20.awk presidents
```

Test Patterns

The test pattern that is matched can be a regular expression, such as that used with **grep**, or it can be a complex mathematical expression. The regular expression is enclosed with slashes, as

/regular-expression/

You can specify a range between two regular expressions by separating them with commas, as

/regular-expression/,*/regular-expression/*

The pattern can also be the keyword **BEGIN** or **END**. The corresponding actions are performed before any input records are read or after all records are read. For example,

```
BEGIN {FS = ":"}
```

sets the field separator to a colon, which is useful for using **awk** with the **/etc/passwd** file. If you had

```
END {print "Number of records is " NR}
```

the number of records in the input would be printed at the end of the file.

The test pattern can include expressions in which variables are tested against numeric values or regular expressions. The numeric testing operators include:

Equality	==
Greater than	>
Less than	<
Greater than or equal to	>=
Less than or equal to	<=
Not equal to	!=

For example,

```
NR > 10 {print}
```

prints all records after the tenth one. The string matching operators test against regular expressions. Their syntax is

Matches   *field ~ regular-expression*
Does not match   *field !~ regular-expression*

For example,

```
$2 ~ /Adams/ {print}
```

prints those records whose second field contains **Adams**. The regular expression can include matching only at the beginning of a field (^) and matching at the end of a field ($).

Tests can be logically combined using the boolean AND, OR, and NOT operators.

AND   &&
OR ||
NOT   !

For example,

```
NR < 10 || NR > 20 {print}
```

prints records before the tenth or after the twentieth.

Workout awk

1. Write the program **count.awk**.

   ```
   END { print NR}
   ```

2. Run the program on **one.doc**.

   ```
   $ awk -f count.awk one.doc
   ```

3. Try the same thing as an immediate program.

```
$ awk 'END { print NR}' one.doc
```

4. Create a file containing simulated expense categories and amounts. Call it **expense.data**: for example,

```
Auto     55.33
Plane    1022.12
Meals    12.44
Auto     12.10
Meals    15.22
```

5. Create an **awk** program that will process this file and check for high expenses. The file (say **expense-high.awk**) might look like

```
$2 > 1000. { print "High expense " $0}
```

6. Run the program on **expense.data**.

```
awk -f expense-high.awk expense.data
```

Print Formatting

If you print fields or strings separated by spaces, the fields are concatenated together. That is, there are no characters between them. If you use a comma, the fields are separated by the output field separator (**OFS**), which is the space character by default. Each time you print, the output ends with the output record separator (**ORS**), which is defaulted to the <new-line>. You can set the value of **OFS** and **ORS** to be anything you want.[2]

Variables and Expressions

You can set and test values that are expressions. Operators used in expressions include the standard arithmetic operators (*****, **/**, **+**, **-**) and

---

[2] For C programmers, there are also versions of **sprintf** and **printf**.

the modulus operator (%), which is the remainder when the first operand is divided by the second. [3] For example,

```
BEGIN {adam_count = 0}
$2 ~ /Adam/ { adam_count = adam_count + 1}
END {print "Count of adams is " adam_count}
```

The variable **adam-count** is set to zero at the beginning of the file. Each time the first field contains **Adam**, the value is added to 1 and placed back in itself. Then at the end of the file, the value is printed out.

If you want to perform multiple statements in an action, separate them with semicolons (;) for example,

```
BEGIN {adam_count = 0; washington_count = 0}
```

Fields can be specified not only with a constant, but also with the $ symbol, as $*variable* and $*expression*. For example,

```
{count = 1; print $count, $(count + 3) }
```

is the same as

```
{print $1, $4}
```

awk tells the usage of a variable by its context. For example, if a variable is used with a + operator, it is treated as a numeric variable. If a variable is used with ~, it is treated as a string.

---

[3] C programmers should note that awk has additional operators that are familiar (++, --, +=, -=, *=, /=, %=).

Workout awk variables

1. Create **expense.data** from the preceding workout if you have not already done so.
2. Create an **awk** program that will process this file and total up the amounts. The file (say, **expense.awk**) could look like

```
        { sum = sum + $2 }
END     {print "Total expenses " sum}
```

3. Run the program on **expense.data**.

```
awk -f expense.awk expense.data
```

4. Create an **awk** program that will process this file and total the amount in each category. The file (say, **expense-breakdown.awk**) could look like

```
$1 ~ /Auto/    { auto_exp = auto_exp + $2 }
$1 ~ /Plane/   { plane_exp = plane_exp + $2}
$1 ~ /Meals/   { meals_exp = meals_exp + $2}
END            {print "Meals " meals_exp; print\
               "Auto " auto_exp; print "Plane"\
               plane_exp}
```

5. Run the program on **expense.data**.

```
awk -f expense-breakdown.awk expense.data
```

Functions

There are several functions that are provided as part of **awk**. The functions can be used in either the test pattern or the action. They include:

Number of characters in *string*	**length**(*string*)
Integer portion of *number*	**int**(*number*)
Index of *a-string* in *another-string*	**index**(*another-string*, *a-string*)
Substring of a string	**substr**(*string*, *starting-position*, *length*)

For example,

```
length($1) > 10 { print "Long last name " $1}
```

prints any record whose first field is longer than 10 characters.

Associative Arrays

With typical programming languages, there are variables that are arrays of values. A numeric value, called the index, is used to pick out a particular value within the array.

awk has associative arrays. The index to this type of array is any type of value. To create an associative array, you just make a reference to a variable using an index. The syntax is

```
array[string] = value
```

For example,

```
phone["bill"] = "555-1212"
```

sets the value of **phone** for **"Bill"** to **"555-1212"**.

You loop through the elements of an array using the **for** statement in an action. Its syntax is

```
for (index-name in array) statement
```

For each element in *array*, the value of *index-name* is set to the value of the index and then *statement* is executed. For example, if you want to keep some phone numbers in an array and print them out, you could code

```
BEGIN {                                        \
      phone["bill"] = "555-1212"; \
      phone["sam"] = "555-7575";   \
      phone["harry"] = "555-2323" \
      }
      . . .
END   { for (name in phone) print name, phone[name] }
```

The value of **name** will successively get the value **"bill"**, **"sam"**, and **"harry"** each time through the loop.

A supplied function can split a string with delimiters into elements in an array. Its syntax is

```
split(string, array, delimiter)
```

Each element in *array* gets a piece of the original string.

Workout   awk associative arrays

---

1. Create the file called **expense.data** if you have not done so in previous workouts.

2. Create an **awk** program that will process this file and total up the amounts in each category. The file (say, **expense-array.awk**) could look like

```
    { expense[$1] = expense[$1] + $2 }
END { for (name in expense) print name, expense[name] }
```

3. Run the program on **expense.data**.

```
awk -f expense-array.awk expense.data
```

4. Try the following program, call it **word.awk**,which counts the number of words in a file.

```
{ split($0, words, " "); \
    for (i in words) word_count[words[i]] = \
    word_count[words[i]] + 1 }
END   { for (word in word_count) print word,\
    word_count[word] ) }
```

5. Run it with one of the files, say **one.doc**.

```
awk -f word.awk one.doc
```

CONTROL STATEMENTS

If you have programmed in C, you will enjoy using the numerous control statements that can be part of the actions in **awk**. The statements include the ones in Table 15-1. You can find examples of these in the **awk** documentation.

FOR FURTHER INFORMATION

Aho, A. V., Kernighan, B. W., and Weinberger, P. J. 1988. *The AWK Programming Language*. Addison Wesley.

Aho, A. V., Kernighan, B. W., and Weinberger, P. J. 1978. *Awk: A Pattern Scanning and Processing Language*, 2nd ed. UNIX Documentation Set.

TABLE 15–1 **awk** Control Statements

```
if (condition)
    statement
else
    statement
while (condition)
    statement
break
continue
next
exit  (to END)
return expression
for (initial-expression;  test-expression;
    increment-expression)
    statement
```

Dougherty, Dale. 1991. *Sed and Awk.* O'Reilly.

Kernighan, Brian W., and Pike, Rob. 1984. *The UNIX Programming Environment.* Englewood Cliffs, N. J.: Prentice Hall. Includes programming the Bourne shell, **awk**, and other tools.

COMMAND SUMMARY

Run program file	**awk -f** program-file data-file
Run in-line program	**awk** 'program' data-file
Statement form	test-pattern {action}
Assignment	variable = value
Fields	$number
Entire record	$0
Built-in variables	
Number fields	**NF**
Number of the record	**NR**
Record separator	**RS**
Field separator	**FS**
Output record separator	**ORS**
Output field separator	**OFS**

Patterns
    Beginning of file   **BEGIN**
    End of file   **END**
    Regular expression   */regular-expression/*
    Range   */regular-expression/,/regular-expression/*
    Pattern comparison   *field ~ regular-expression*
                                  field !~ regular-expression

Operators
    Arithmetic   ***, /, +, -, %**
    Comparison operators   **==, !=, >, >=, <, <=**
    Logical operators   **&&, ||, !**
Functions
    Number of characters
        in *string*   **length**(*string*)
    Integer portion of *number* **int**(*number*)
    Index of *a-string* in   **index**(*another-string, a- string*)
        another-string
    Substring of a string   **substr**(*string, starting-position, length*)
    Split string into array   **split**(*string, array, delimiter*)
Associative arrays
    Referencing   *array*[*string*]
    For loop   **for** (*index-name* **in** *array*) *statement*

16 | OTHER TOPICS

It ain't over yet

This chapter covers a few miscellaneous programs that you may want to use sometime. It also explores a couple of interesting facets of UNIX.

FILE ARCHIVING: tar

You can buy utilities for MS-DOS such as packing and compression, and backup programs such as **PKZIP**. Programs with similar functions are already part of UNIX. The file archiving program combines sets of files into a single file. It was originally used to write files out to a tape drive for archiving, which gives it its name: **tar** (tape archiver). However, you can use it for a number of different purposes. The syntax is

```
tar options filename(s)
```

The default output of **tar** is the system tape drive, but you can alter that with the **-f** *filename* option. To create a **tar** file, use the **-c** option, as

```
tar -cf backup.tar *.bak
```

You can see what is on the **tar** file with the table of contents option (**-t**); for example,

```
tar -tf backup.tar
```

To extract the files, you use the **-x** option, such as

```
tar -xf backup.tar one.bak
```

If you specify a directory name, **tar** will recursively save or extract all the files in that directory.

FILE ARCHIVING: cpio

You can also archive files with the **cpio** program. It works slightly differently from the **tar** program. You provide it a list of files to be archived on the standard input. Usually, you use **find** or **ls** to output the filenames, but you can just create a list of filenames with a text editor. It writes the archive file to standard output. The syntax for using **cpio** for output is

```
cpio -o < list-of-filenames > archive-name
```

For example, if you wanted to store all the files in your current directory, use

```
ls | cpio -o > all.arc
```

To retrieve a file, you use

```
cpio -i pattern < archive-name
```

Files whose names match *pattern* will be retrieved from *archive-name* and copied to the current directory. If you do not specify a *pattern*, all files will be copied. For example,

```
cpio -i one.doc < all.arc
```

will retrieve the **one.bak** file. To retrieve all the files you would use

```
cpio -i < all.arc
```

If you want to list the table of contents of the files, use the **-t** option, as

```
cpio -it pattern < archive-name
```

COMPRESSION

You might want to compress a **tar** file or any other file to save space. UNIX provides standard **compress** and **uncompress** programs. The **compress** program creates a compressed file with a **.Z** appended on the end. The **uncompress** program decompresses a **.Z** file back into a normal file. The syntax for these programs is

```
compress original-filename
uncompress original-filename.Z
```

For example,

```
compress backup.tar
```

creates a file called **backup.tar.Z**;

```
uncompress backup.tar.Z
```

uncompresses the file into **backup.tar**.

FILE-TYPE DETERMINATION

As explained in Chapter 2, UNIX does not use filenames to identify the type of file. Before running **cat** on an unknown file, you should determine whether it is an executable program or a text file. The **file** program examines the files whose names you give and outputs its determination as to what the type of each file is. It can distinguish between text files and executable files. For example,

```
file one.doc
```

will output

```
one.doc ASCII text
```

SPELLING CHECKER

The **spell** program checks words in a text file and output words it does not find in a standard list (**/usr/dict/words**) and/or a user-provided list. It applies modifications to the words (as common prefixes and suffixes), before determining that a word does not match. It ignores **nroff** and **troff** commands. The syntax is

> **spell** *filenames*

CALENDAR

Two programs deal with the days. The **cal** program prints out a calendar for a month. The **calendar** program is a reminder service. It looks through a file called **calendar** in the current directory or home directory and prints out lines containing the current date or the next day's date. It can even send you mail regarding the events on dates. The **calendar** file can contain references to other files, such as a common schedule file.

CALCULATOR

Two interactive calculators are available on many systems. The desk calculator (**dc**) is a stack-oriented calculator that provides the standard operations with unlimited precision arithmetic. The **bc** program provides a C-like syntax interpreter with unlimited precision arithmetic. It reads input from the standard input or from a file and uses **dc** to perform the operations.

LEAVING PROCESSES RUNNING

When you log off a terminal or hangup (if on a modem), all background processes that you have started with the Bourne shell are terminated. To avoid this, you can use the **nohup** command, as

> **nohup**   *command* &

The *command* will continue to run in the background until it is finished, even if you log off.

With the C shell, a process that is running in foreground can be terminated if you hang up. Background processes continue to run even if you hang up. The **nohup** statement is part of the C shell rather than a separate command. If you use

> **nohup**   *command*

then *command* does not terminate if you hang up.

PATH FOR AN EXECUTABLE FILE

The value of $PATH (or $path) gives the list of directories to search to find a particular executable. It may be useful to determine in which directory a particular program that you are running is located. The **which** command reports the directory in which a command is located. The syntax is

    which command

For example,

    which sh

may report

    /bin/sh

DIFFERENT NAMES FOR SAME FILES

MS-DOS keeps information about the contents of a file with the filename in the directory. Each file is uniquely identified by a name. In contrast, UNIX stores in the directory the name of the file and just a numeric index which represents where to find information about the file contents. This file information is kept in an "inode", or information node. The numeric index is called the "inode number". The relationship between a filename and its inode number is called a link, in the sense that the name in the directory is linked to the file.

DIAGRAM Inodes

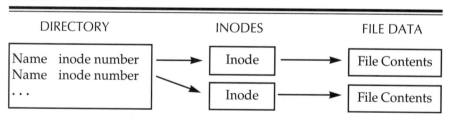

Because of this organization, it is possible for two names in the same directory or different directories to have the same inode number. Regardless of which name you use to specify the file, the same inode and the same contents will be accessed.

The **ln** command creates a link to an existing file. Its syntax is

```
ln existing-file new-name
```

For example,

```
ln one.doc some-other.doc
```

creates a link for **some-other.doc** to the same file as **one.doc**.

DIAGRAM Example (after the command has executed)

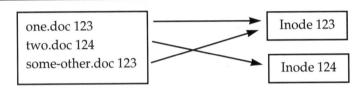

Once you have made the link, you can use either

```
cat one.doc
```

or

```
cat some-other.doc
```

to list the file. Links made with this command are called "hard links". Once the link is created, you cannot tell which directory entry was the original one.

When you do a long listing with **ls**, one of the columns contains the number of links to the file. This is the number of directory entries that reference the inode associated with the file.

When you use **rm** to remove a file, the system removes the directory entry associated with the name. If the name was the only link to the file, the inode and the disk blocks where contents of the file were kept are made available for use by other files. If at least one other directory entry (link) to the file exists, the inode and the contents are not affected.

You cannot make a hard link between files on different file systems. A file system is the equivalent of a MS-DOS hard disk partition. BSD permits you to make a "soft link", which can cross file systems. A soft link is actually a special file that contains the name of the file that is referenced. The syntax for creating a soft link is

```
ln -s existing-file new-name
```

For example,

```
ln -s one.doc another.doc
```

creates a soft link called **another.doc**. This file appears in the directory listing with **l** as its type. A reference to **another.doc** will be translated into a reference to **one.doc**. If you remove **one.doc**, the actual file will be deleted, since soft links are not counted in determining whether to keep the contents of a file. If **one.doc** is deleted, the reference in **another.doc** will no longer be valid.

DIRECTORY CONTENTS

A detailed look at how files are organized in UNIX may help explain further the differences between it and the MS-DOS organization. In MS-DOS, each directory entry contains a filename, a modification date, attributes, size in bytes, and a pointer to the starting cluster (group of disk sectors) in the file allocation table. Each MS-DOS file is unique. The CHKDSK program determines if two files contain the same allocated clusters (disk sectors).

When a file is deleted in MS-DOS, a single unique character is put in the first character of the filename entry so that the entry does not appear in the directory list. The disk sectors for the file are not reused until a new file is created or an existing file is extended. This permits the UNDELETE program to work. To restore a file, you need to supply the first character.

With UNIX, each entry in the directory contains a filename and an inode (information node) number. Each file system has particular disk blocks on which it keeps all current and available inodes for that system. The inode number is an index into this area. Inode numbers start at 0 on each file system. The first two numbers are used for system purposes, so the inode for the root directory (/) is number 2.

Each inode contains the file permissions; the user and group owner ids; creation, modification, and last access times; the size; and pointers to which disk blocks contain the data for the file. The **ls** command prints out this information for the filenames requested.

Multiple directory entries can contain the same inode number. The inode itself contains the number of entries linked to it. If a directory entry is deleted, the link count is decremented. When the link count goes to zero, the inode is marked as available and the data sectors in the file are freed. The data cannot be reclaimed.

The move program (**mv**) changes just the filename for a file in a directory. If a different directory is specified, the entry in the original directory is deleted and another entry is made in the new directory. The actual contents of the file is not copied, just the inode number.

FOR FURTHER INFORMATION

Check the **man** pages for each command or the references in the Epilogue.

COMMAND SUMMARY

Different names for same files
    Hard link   **ln** *existing-file new-name*
    Soft link   **ln -s** *existing-file new-name*
File archiving   **tar** *options filename(s)*
    Filename   **-f** *filename*
    Creating   **-c**
    Table of contents   **-t**
    Extracting   **-x**
File archiving
    Creating   **cpio -o** < *filename* > *archive-name*
    Table of contents   **cpio -it** *pattern* < *archive-name*
    Extracting   **cpio -i** *pattern* < *archive-name*
File compression   **compress** *filename*
File decompression   **uncompress** *compressed-filename*
File type determination   **file** *filename(s)*
Spelling checker   **spell** *filenames*
Calendar   **cal**
Calendar reminder   **calendar**
Leaving processes running   **nohup** *command* **& (sh)**
                          nohup *command* **(csh)**

Path for executable file   **which** *command*
Calculator   **bc** and **dc**

EPILOGUE

This is not the end, but just a beginning

The directions in which you can explore UNIX are numerous. You can explore text processing, shell scripts, networks, and more. If you are a programmer, you can try out the C compiler and the interface to the operating system. You could program a socket, a stream, or other interprocess communication. Best wishes for your future explorations.

Bach, M. J. 1986. *The Design of the UNIX Operating System.* Englewood Cliffs, N.J.: Prentice Hall.

Bell Labs. 1987. *UNIX System Readings and Applications,* Vol. I. Englewood Cliffs, N.J.: Prentice Hall.

Bell Labs. 1987. *UNIX System Readings and Applications,* Vol. II. Englewood Cliffs, N.J.: Prentice Hall.

Leffler, S. J., McKusick, M. K., Karels, M. J., and Quarterman, J. S. 1989. *The Design and Implementation of the 4.3BSD Operating System.* Reading, Mass.: Addison-Wesley. Internal design of BSD.

Stevens, W. R. 1990. *UNIX Network Programming.* Englewood Cliffs, N.J.: Prentice Hall.

APPENDIX: MS-DOS/UNIX COMMAND COMPARISON

Following is a list of MS-DOS and the closest comparative UNIX command or features. Commands that are not applicable in UNIX are listed as "N/A". Page references are given for commands and features described in this book. Features for which pages are listed as "man" should be looked up in your system manual.

MS-DOS	UNIX	Page Reference
ANSI.SYS	`TERM=`	32
APPEND	N/A	
ASSIGN	`link`	221
ATTRIB	`chmod`	14
AUTOEXEC.BAT	`.profile` or `.login`	111, 135
	`/etc/rc` (BSD)	172
	`/etc/inittab` (System V)	172
BACKUP	`dump` (BSD)	168
	`backup` (System V)	168
BREAK	`trap` (shell script)	130
BUFFER= (config.sys)	configuration	168
CALL	script name	78
CHCP	N/A	
CHDIR	`cd`	23
CHKDSK	`fsck`	167

CLS	`clear`	
COMMAND	`sh, csh, ksh`	27
COMP	`cmp`	104
COPY	`cp`	18
COUNTRY	N/A	
CTTY	(I/O redirection)	33
DATE	`date` (read-only)	105
DEBUG	`dbx`	
DEL	`rm`	20
DEVICE =	I/O drivers	173
DEVICEHIGH	N/A	
DIR	`ls`	15
DISKCOMP	N/A	
DISKCOPY	`tar`	216
DOS=	N/A	
DOSKEY	`history` (`csh, ksh`)	131, 136
DOSSHELL	X-Windows	
DRIVPARM	`/etc/disktab`	165
ECHO	`echo`	77
EDIT	`vi`	38
EDLIN	`ed`	38
EMM386	N/A	
EXE2BIN	N/A	
EXIT	<control-D> or `logout`	8
EXPAND	`compress` and `uncompress`	218
FASTOPEN	N/A	
FC	`diff`	190
FCBS	configuration	172
FDISK	`chpt`	
FILES=	configuration	172
FIND	`grep`	89
FOR	`for` (shell scripts)	121, 148
FORMAT	`newfs`	
GOTO	other shell script control features	116, 143, 154
GRAFTABL	N/A	
GRAPHICS	N/A	
HELP	`man`	9
IF	`if` (shell scripts)	118, 147
INSTALL=	`/etc/rc` (BSD)	111, 135
	`/etc/inittab` (System V)	172
JOIN	`mount`	165
KEYB	`TERM=`	32
LABEL	N/A	
LASTDRIVE	Number of file systems mounted	165

LOADHIGH		N/A	
MEM		`vmstat`	175
MIRROR		not standard—supplied by vendors	
MKDIR		`mkdir`	23
MODE	(printers)	device drivers	174
	(terminals)	`/etc/ttys` (BSD)	172
		`/etc/inittab` (System V)	172
		`stty`	30
	(codepages)	N/A	
MORE		`more`	3
NLSFUNC		N/A [supported by NLS functions (XOpen)]	
PATH		`PATH` environmental variables	28
PAUSE		`read` (shell scripts)	113, 142
PRINT		`lp, lpr`	21
PROMPT		`PS1, prompt` shell variable	110, 135
QBASIC		Basic may be supplied by vendor	
RECOVER		`fsck`	167
REM		`#` (shell script)	83
RENAME		`mv`	19
REPLACE		`cp`	18
RESTORE		`restore, restore`	168
RMDIR		`rmdir`	24
SET		`export` (sh, ksh)	32
		`setenv` (csh)	32
SETVER		N/A	
SHARE		`flock, lockf`—system calls	
SHELL		`/etc/passwd` entry	59, 162
SHIFT		`shift` (shell script)	113, 142
SORT		`sort`	95
STACKS		N/A	
SUBST		`link`	221
SWITCHES		`TERM=`	32
SYS		Installation procedure	172
TIME		`date` (read-only)	105
TREE		N/A	
TYPE		`cat`	21
UNDELETE		N/A	
UNFORMAT		N/A	
VER		N/A	
VERIFY		N/A	
VOL		N/A	
XCOPY		`cp -r`	18
<control-Z>		<control-D>	3

INDEX

228